W9-CUJ-152

THE IMPERFECT COMMONWEALTH

A failing in the past has been that we have tended to conceive of it as a perfect Commonwealth. In the Seventies we should replace that concept with that of the imperfect Commonwealth. All we can hope to achieve, as in every other human endeavour, is a less imperfect Commonwealth, but one which will always remain an imperfect Commonwealth.

S. RAJARATNAM, *Foreign Minister of Singapore, on the last day of the Commonwealth Heads of Government meeting in Singapore, 1971.*

BY THE SAME AUTHOR

Partners in Adventure   1960
The Commonwealth Challenge   1962
Commonwealth for a Colour-Blind World   1965
The Commonwealth at Work   1969

TO RACHEL

whose father was so dedicated to the
Commonwealth of tomorrow.

The Imperfect Commonwealth

DEREK INGRAM

REX COLLINGS
LONDON
1977

|||

First published in Great Britain by
Rex Collings Ltd
69 Marylebone High Street, London W1

Derek Ingram 1977

ISBN 0860360490

Typesetting by Malvern Typesetting Services
Printed in Great Britain by
Billing and Sons Ltd
Guildford, London and Worcester

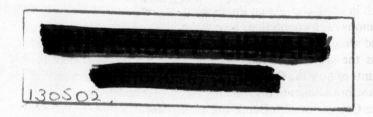

130502,

FOREWORD

SHRIDATH RAMPHAL
Commonwealth Secretary-General

Derek Ingram calls his book *The Imperfect Commonwealth*, and the adjective is well applied. If the Commonwealth, and the world it serves, were perfect, there might be no need for organizations within which the nations can work together and learn to understand each other. That remedy for its own imperfections is what the Commonwealth offers to its members and to mankind.

I became Secretary-General of the Commonwealth in 1975, and for ten years before that, in public life in my own country, I was a close participant in Commonwealth affairs. Over all that time I have come to know Derek Ingram as a tireless and perceptive commentator on international affairs in general, and on the Commonwealth in particular. As an Englishman, his own and his country's Commonwealth connections have given him a deep understanding of and sympathy for the problems of the Commonwealth's peoples across the globe. It is most valuable to have collected here his accounts of how the Commonwealth developed during the years of its transformation into the still evolving form it has today.

The Commonwealth Derek Ingram chronicles as a sympathetic observer is not at all points that which I have known as an insider. The pains of transformation have at times been greater: the achievements sometimes significant in different ways. But his facts tend to be extremely accurate, and his opinions—friendly and constructive always—are his own. Above all, his knowledge of the Commonwealth has tended to confirm him in the view that it matters, and that its place in the world, while very different from what it was only ten years ago, is secure.

I am sure he is right. I only regret that so many commentators do not take the trouble to ascertain the persuasive facts that so strongly support his view. Because the Commonwealth of today is such a new creation, it may be inevitable that it is less well understood than it deserves to be. Derek Ingram's collection of studies is a real contribution to putting the record straight.

Contents

Introduction

FOR THOSE OF us who have argued throughout the last 20 years that the Commonwealth is an association of nations that is of value in the modern world and, furthermore, is likely to survive and to move towards a more important role than that it has performed so far, the road has not been smooth. Reactions have ranged from the cynical and dismissive to expressions of apathy and disbelief. Few in the mid-Sixties were prepared to accept that the Commonwealth *would* survive. The Commonwealth was regularly given a premature ritual burial by press and radio and the published commentaries of many learned and less learned observers are littered with its obituaries. Until quite recently every summit conference was seen as likely to be the last.

In the Sixties anyone who wrote a book on the Commonwealth was putting his head on the block. Quite apart from the majority view that the Commonwealth had no future, there was the actuality that anything written today was quite likely to be out of date on the morrow. Faith and a general feeling that all would be well in the end were fair enough, but one never knew when the next shock might come or where it might come from; whatever argument might be put up there was always the chance that one of the twenty or thirty member-countries of the Commonwealth could produce (and sometimes did) an incident or a development that was the exception to the rule you had tried to argue applied.

Predictions about the Commonwealth, particularly about events in certain areas of it, were highly dangerous to make. I put my own head on the block four times by writing books about it during this period and on numerous other occasions when I discussed the Commonwealth in a variety of magazine and newspaper articles. By no means everything worked out, but some things did.

In his *Survey of Commonwealth Affairs* Professor Bruce Miller said that Commonwealth commentators of the Sixties could be divided into those taking four 'sorts of attitude'. These he defined as: Scholarly-contemplative, idealistic-traditional, idealistic-progressive and realistic-optimistic. He suggested that I fell into two categories, moving from the third to the fourth between the beginning and the end of the Sixties. This is probably fair, though I would argue that it is possible to be idealistic and realistic at one and the same time. Some, however, might see that in itself as an idealistic attitude.

For this book I have written a new opening essay and followed it with a compilation of contemporary reports of the Commonwealth story as it unfolded in the immediate post-independence period—that is, after the main period of decolonization in the first half of the Sixties. The heart of the book consists of descriptions and analyses of the four key Heads of Government conferences held between 1969 and 1975, as a result of which the Commonwealth underwent a great transformation.

This book does not set out to give a comprehensive picture of the Commonwealth today, but rather to convey an impression of the way in which it has developed in the years since I wrote my earlier books on the subject and, above all, to give the reader a feel for the atmosphere of Commonwealth meetings and some idea of the scope of the work and influence of the Commonwealth.

It is also intended to serve two other purposes. One is to show how the Commonwealth is seen by those at the top—Presidents, Prime Ministers, Ministers and officials who regularly attend Commonwealth gatherings. The other is to show what the Commonwealth can mean to those who are far more important—the 1,000 million peoples whose lives the Commonwealth must enrich in one way or another if it is to justify its existence.

Most of the material in this book is compiled from articles written for three organizations and I am therefore heavily in debt to the Editor and my other colleagues on the editorial committee of *The Round Table* for permission to republish material originally written for that journal; to the Royal Commonwealth Society for use of articles written for its journal *Commonwealth*; and for my own company, Gemini News Service Ltd. for access to material written during the course of assignments on its behalf. I would also like to thank the Information Division of the Commonwealth Secretariat for their help in assembling some of the material contained herein.

CHAPTER ONE
Towards an Outward-looking Commonwealth

PEOPLE ARE INTERESTING, but on the whole things are a bore. A television screen is a marvel; the people who appear on it are infinitely more appealing. A lunar landing vehicle is a wonder of our age; the men who walk on the moon and the descriptions of what they see and how they live in a capsule in the sky are far more fascinating. A tractor thrills only the most enthusiastic motor mechanic; the man who drives it is a human being whose habits and customs and way of life are of infinite interest.

The Commonwealth as such, like the United Nations, the European Economic Community, the Organization of African Unity and all other international organizations, is a bore. It is nebulous: a collection of unlike countries that exists for not very obvious purposes, that has spawned a large number of organizations with dull-sounding names and even duller-sounding objectives. On closer examination, however, a rather different picture emerges. The Commonwealth is 1,000 million people—a quarter of the population and a quarter of the nations of the world—and the reason it exists is because the co-operation it offers can somehow help to improve and enrich the lives of at least a few of them and hopefully a lot of them. Governments belong to the Commonwealth on a simple hardheaded assessment that there are benefits to be gained from membership for their countries—and for no other reason.

It cannot be said that any country belongs to the Commonwealth today because of historical sentiment. Nor can any government now be said to be trying to exploit the Commonwealth for its own ends; it was once true, particularly in the early Sixties and before, that Britain saw the Commonwealth as something to be manipulated to its advantage, as what follows in these pages sometimes shows. Those days are past. Certainly governments see Commonwealth membership as enhancing their position in the world or as helping to make their own foreign policies distinctive. The Canadians have played a leading role in the Commonwealth in recent years because they believe the special relationship it provides with many developing countries all over the world helps to give Canada a role quite separate from that of the United States, the neighbour to which it is always trying to stop looking over its shoulder.

Tanzania, Zambia, Botswana and other African countries have found themselves equipped with an extra diplomatic network, an added dimension, within which to pursue their aims of bringing

2

about a transition to majority rule in southern Africa; Commonwealth membership gives tiny and geographically isolated Tonga and Western Samoa more of an opportunity to make their views known about the moves towards a new international economic order which are engaging the big powers and the poor and rich worlds; on quite another level, India, with Commonwealth help, is able to develop better ways of packaging and launching its goods so that they are more competitive in the slick, sharp markets of the rich world.

There was much confusion in men's minds about the Commonwealth in the turbulent Sixties—and not surprisingly. The Association entered the decade with a membership of ten countries, which included only Ghana from Black Africa and no Caribbean representation, and ended it with 28 members, after the withdrawal of one of its original members, South Africa. By 1970 it was a totally different body from what it had been in 1960. The cosy, polite Prime Ministers' conferences of the Fifties when only India, Pakistan and Ceylon represented the Third World, had been replaced by often stormy sessions of Heads of Government that were showing signs of becoming formalized.

The change had taken place so rapidly that countries used the threat of withdrawal from the Commonwealth as a means of putting pressure on the British; not yet had the fact been grasped that the Commonwealth was becoming a multi-lateral association, rather than just a series of bilateral relationships with Britain. For its part Britain did not seem to understand the nature of the organization to which it had almost unwittingly given birth. There was no worked out pattern about the formation of the Commonwealth as it is today; in the Fifties and Sixties one independence ceremony followed on from another, and as it did so each new country decided to remain in the Commonwealth, now as a full member instead of as a colonial appendage of Britain.

When Harold Wilson became Prime Minister in 1964 he and the Labour Party, which had been at the forefront of the agitation in Britain for decolonization, now found themselves strangely out of touch with what had happened partly as a result of their own efforts. They had not grasped that what was now forming was not a Commonwealth-cum-Empire in which Britain would still remain the most influential member. If Wilson had understood the change he would never have attempted to use the Commonwealth to curry support at home by proposing a Commonwealth peace mission to

3

Vietnam—a proposition suddenly launched on an unwitting, un-suspecting Commonwealth at its summit meeting in London in 1965.

Only as a result of hard experience over several years, starting with the collapse of that mission even before it started and con-tinuing with the repeated failure of British manoeuvrings over Rhodesia, did British Ministers learn that the Commonwealth was not going to be another form of Empire through which Britain might remain powerful in many areas of the world.

Those who had seen the Commonwealth as such a device—as something it was not—were soured and turned against it; others who had set their sights too high with the idealistic notions of what the Commonwealth could achieve in terms of race relations, peace-ful solutions to problems like those of Southern Africa and over-ambitious plans for alleviating world poverty, became disillusioned and many of them decided that it was a failure. They had expected far too much of it far too soon.

The Commonwealth was not immune from the strengths and weaknesses of the rest of the world; it was subject to exactly the same strains and stresses. It became plain, as the Seventies came along, that the Commonwealth was, after all, only representative of the whole; a 'sample' of the world, as it is now sometimes called.

Since the Commonwealth connection gave this unlikely mixture of countries so many ready-made links did it not make sense to try to build on such a foundation rather than to destroy what was obviously intrinsically good?

The rather sudden formation of a Commonwealth Secretariat in 1965 as a result of an initiative by Ghana's President Dr Kwame Nkrumah (the fruits of which he never saw in action since he was ousted from power in March 1966), provided the necessary impetus and minimum infrastructure to mould the Commonwealth into its new form. Without a Secretariat that took the administrative running of the Commonwealth out of Whitehall's hands the Commonwealth would certainly have foundered.

Now the way was open for the careful building and expansion of the many non-political fields of activity which must be the foundation of the Commonwealth—specialized technical aid schemes, the setting up of professional centres and provision of opportunities for professional people to develop their careers, the development of programmes for youth that would play their part in trying to prevent the urban drift and to furthering self-help pro-

4

grammes, providing expert advice to countries faced with complex negotiations over their commodities' arrangements, agricultural development and industrialization.

The Commonwealth only just survived. It nearly came to an end in the months following the summit conference in London in September 1966. Withdrawal of an African member country over Rhodesia at that time—very much on the cards on more than one occasion—would have set off a domino effect. In the last analysis it was people like President Julius Nyerere of Tanzania, Prime Ministers Lester Pearson and Pierre Trudeau of Canada, President Kenneth Kaunda of Zambia, and Prime Minister Lee Kuan Yew of Singapore, helped by the first Commonwealth Secretary-General, Arnold Smith, who had the vision to save it from disintegrating. The way in which they did this emerges from the pages that follow.

At a later stage, Pakistan was to leave the Commonwealth without causing even a ripple; an indication of how, by 1972, despite the brinkmanship practised at the Singapore summit only a year before, everyone was much more confident that the Commonwealth would and should survive.

The Singapore meeting of heads of government is seen as the turning point in modern Commonwealth history; certainly it changed attitudes and pointed the Commonwealth in new directions. But the now largely forgotten meeting in London in January 1969 had already begun to restore confidence.

It was at that meeting that the very important Commonwealth figure of Pierre Trudeau first appeared on the scene; a French Canadian who, on his own confession, knew little of Commonwealth affairs when he came to office in 1968. The Canadian role in the Commonwealth, already a key one under John Diefenbaker (Conservative Prime Minister from 1957 to 1963) and Lester Pearson, now became more important than ever under Trudeau. By taking a position midway between that of the other original Commonwealth members, Britain, Australia, and New Zealand, and the new countries, Canada prevented a division between the white and non-white Commonwealth that if it had been allowed to develop could only have proved fatal. Then, by bringing about changes in the style and procedure of Commonwealth Heads of Government meetings, Trudeau pulled the Commonwealth away from moving towards United Nations-style formalization, which also could have led to its eventual demise.

At the Singapore meeting in 1971 the Commonwealth leaders

5

faced up to the question: Do we really want the Commonwealth to go on or not? They were riven by the British decision to sell arms to South Africa, but by now it had become quite clear that the Commonwealth was no longer a British institution. President Nyerere had already demonstrated this in 1965 when Tanzania had broken relations with Britain but remained a member of the Commonwealth—the first time such a situation had arisen. The Heads of Government at Singapore also had in their minds the significant body of work that was being continuously undertaken at a functional level; they knew the value of their own close personal relationships that had developed largely because of the existence of the Commonwealth. Did they want to throw all this away and with it the potential for future good?

In the end, after agonizing hours of discussion alone, without even officials present, they decided that they did not. No one walked out of the Singapore meeting, as it had been suggested they might do, and everyone stayed to learn some lessons. The British would say that in their tough stand on South African arms they had shown that Britain was an independent country, too, and would pursue its own foreign policy in the way it wanted; too often in the Sixties, argued Whitehall, it had been at the receiving end of criticism from the developing countries. Now, Mr Heath said when he came away, Britain had stood its ground and would do what it thought was right in the national interest. In fact it had learned at Singapore that a different policy from the one he had advocated was in the national interest: in the months after Singapore Britain quietly retreated from its position on South African arms sales.

The developing countries, for their part, learned that Commonwealth conferences were not the place for posturing and reading out long texts for domestic consumption; they were for dialogue across the table, and cut and thrust of debate. The need to change the procedural style of the conference was clear.

Another cloud hung over the Commonwealth in the Sixties which convinced many commentators that the association could not last—the whole question of British entry into the European Economic Community. Many people could not see how a Britain in the EEC could possibly be compatible with the existence of the Commonwealth; many ardent pro-Europeans in Britain persisted in arguing that Britain must choose between Europe and the Commonwealth. The either-or case was always false, but it was potentially damaging and served further to confuse the concept of

6

Commonwealth in many minds.

The idea that the Commonwealth was really still the Empire and that Britain was the centre of the Commonwealth under another name, coupled with a complete failure to foresee the way the Commonwealth was developing, led to the view that the abolition of imperial preference and the derogation of some British sovereignty under the terms of the Treaty of Rome were not in line with the continuance of the Commonwealth. In fact, trade patterns were rapidly changing in any case and, Commonwealth or no Commonwealth, imperial preference was plainly not likely to survive many years.

Another mistake that stoked the anti-Commonwealth argument was that the EEC would quite rapidly develop into a political and federal union. Just as some Commonwealth idealists were carried away in the early Sixties on ideas of a tightly-knit, cohesive Commonwealth that might have common economic and foreign policies so 'good Europeans' envisaged a similar cohesiveness for Europe. Events have shown what should always have been obvious: that a United States of Europe lies in the far distant future and that European countries, like all others in the world, are jealous of their sovereignty and will part with it only in tiny doses.

All the same, in the years after Britain's first application to join Europe in 1961 Commonwealth countries, rich and poor, *were* nervous of their economic future once Britain joined Europe and many were fierce in their arguments against British membership. The long period when Britain was kept out of Europe was useful in one respect: Commonwealth countries had plenty of time to begin to rearrange their already changing trade patterns so that their economies were not endangered. When Britain finally joined in 1973 it was with the blessing of the entire Commonwealth and it has since become clear that British membership of Europe has in no way diminished the value of the Commonwealth; it in fact enhances the Commonwealth that the association now has a member which has its feet inside the European door. By means of the Lomé Convention, negotiated as a direct result of British membership, all developing countries which are signatories have a say (even if not a very big say) in Europe's relations with the developing world.

The Commonwealth Heads of Government conference in Ottawa in 1973 opened a new chapter in the history of the Commonwealth. A better political atmosphere had developed; everyone now had a clearer idea of the nature of the Common-

7

wealth's limitations and potentialities. It was a meeting that con- solidated the Commonwealth, during which there was real debate across the table and where the disruptions of the Sixties and the brinkmanship of Singapore seemed quite out of place, and this mood was carried on to the next meeting in Kingston, Jamaica, in 1975.

The harmony at Ottawa and Kingston was helped by the fact that the leaders of Australia and New Zealand were now much more in tune with the modern Commonwealth than their predecessors. Australia had suffered from the fact that Sir Robert Menzies had imprinted on generations of Australians the picture of an imperial Commonwealth and this tradition was carried through succeeding Prime Ministers of the Liberal-Country Party Government. Labour's Gough Whitlam, controversial as he turned out to be domestically, took Australia out into centre ground on foreign affairs alongside Canada. Norman Kirk, the Labour Prime Minister of New Zealand, who came to office at the same time, did likewise and Wallace Rowling, who succeeded on Kirk's death, continued the policy. Now Conservative governments have returned to both countries, but the stated changes in the attitude to Commonwealth affairs have remained under the new governments. There is not much going back in this respect. Certain aspects of foreign policy may be less acceptable to some of the developing world, but not enough to cause serious Commonwealth disruption.

For their part, many of the newer Commonwealth countries had as a result of their experience moved into quieter diplomatic methods and this had made for a greater degree of harmony in the Commonwealth as a whole.

Today, with a Commonwealth of thirty-six members, political decolonization is all but complete. Apart from one or two small territories, the only major potential members are Zimbabwe and Namibia.*

But *economic* decolonization is only just beginning and the Commonwealth in the next decade is bound to become deeply in- volved in this new chapter. At the Kingston meeting the Common- wealth became the first body of nations embracing rich and poor

---

* The Solomon Islands become independent in 1978. The independence of Belize (British Honduras) is held up because of territorial threats by Guatemala. Other eventual full members are Bermuda, Brunei (currently in a special relationship with Britain that fits it into no category), the remaining Caribbean associated states—St Vincent, Montserrat, St Kitts-Nevis, St Lucia and Dominica—and the Gilbert Islands and Tuvalu. Hong Kong and Gibraltar are special cases.

countries to take a hard look at the need for a new international economic order and all that that entailed. Hitherto, groups of rich and poor had met on a number of occasions to discuss the subject, but each separately. The action taken at Kingston and subsequent developments underlined ways in which the Commonwealth is increasingly working as an outgoing influence in international affairs.

At Kingston the Commonwealth began to break out of its boundaries; it showed that it was now by no means an exclusive body, but one that was working to complement other international organizations and particularly the United Nations. As proof of this new trend, the Commonwealth Secretariat was given observer status at the United Nations General Assembly in 1976.

The Commonwealth Experts Group of ten men set up at Kingston to explore ways of moving towards a new international economic order was given the task of producing a preliminary report in time for the United Nations Seventh Special Session in September 1975. This it did and the report proved a valuable help to the debate. Subsequently it produced a further report for UNCTAD Four at Nairobi. In this way the Commonwealth is contributing its collective knowhow and wisdom to the general international scene.

Thus the Commonwealth is moving into a new stage of its role as an international association. During the Sixties it was understandably involved in its own problems; it was a matter of sheer survival as it weathered storms over such problems as Rhodesia. But that phase is now over and the Commonwealth has been turning itself into a body of nations which increasingly works within the greater whole. The Commonwealth has been steadily realizing that its work can help and stretch into all the regional organizations like the EEC, the Association of South East Asian nations (ASEAN), the Caribbean Community (CARICOM), and so forth, as well as into Francophone associations and, most importantly into the United Nations.

With most international associations it has links. During the Paris North-South dialogue talks inaugurated by President Giscard d'Estaing in 1975 at least two or three Commonwealth countries have been members of each of the commissions set up. More than a quarter of the membership of the Organization of African Unity (OAU) are Commonwealth countries. The South Pacific Forum is almost all Commonwealth. Two of the five ASEAN countries are

9

Commonwealth. Commonwealth countries such as Trinidad and Guyana are now members of the Organization of American States (OAS). Commonwealth countries are in the majority in the recently formed Economic Community of West African States (ECOWAS). Two-thirds of Commonwealth countries belong to the Non-Aligned Movement; most of them are in the Group of 77, and so forth. A quarter of the membership of the United Nations are Commonwealth countries. Through the Secretariat the Commonwealth is able to co-ordinate and increase its links with all these regional and international bodies and to work alongside and in a complementary manner to them.

It is little realized just how much Commonwealth liaison has been built up in recent years with outside bodies. The Secretariat has observer status at the regular meetings of GATT and at meetings of the Council's standing committees. UNESCO gave the Secretariat observer status long ago—in 1967. The Secretariat is an observer at meetings of the World Bank and the International Monetary Fund (IMF), at the International Maritime Consultative Organization (IMCO), the UN Food and Agricultural Organization (FAO), UNCTAD, and the Law of the Sea conferences. Meetings of Commonwealth ministers take place before or during conferences such as those of the World Health Assembly and the FAO.

For several years meetings of Permanent Representatives of Commonwealth countries at the United Nations in New York did not take place. There had been a period in the early Sixties when they met regularly, but the custom lapsed during the turbulent years of Commonwealth relations. With the recently improved political mood among the Commonwealth countries all that' has changed; Commonwealth representatives now meet in New York when there is an issue about which they wish to hear each other's views.* Delegates take turns in acting as convenor. They it was who suggested Commonwealth countries should jointly sponsor the resolution at the UN General Assembly in October 1976 proposing observer status.

This will help the Secretariat to work more closely with the UN and its specialized agencies, and, as the Commonwealth secretary-general, Shridath Ramphal, has put it, show the Commonwealth to be an outward-looking association supportive of the UN and in the service of the wider international community.

* Britain's Labour Foreign and Commonwealth Secretary, Mr James Callaghan, was in part responsible for the revival of the meetings in New York.

Thus the Commonwealth is today becoming recognized by the international community as an increasingly significant body and many member-countries are beginning to find that of all the international organizations to which they belong the Commonwealth is one that seems more practical, less bureaucratic, much more informal than most.

The Commonwealth, rather than becoming irrelevant as many people used to suggest and some still do, is in fact becoming more relevant and particularly in its importance in the context of the new international economic order which, whether the industrialized world likes it or not, will somehow have to be worked out over the next decade or two.

CHAPTER TWO

The Secretariat: Born in the Nick of Time

The idea of a Secretariat for the Commonwealth, which quite unexpectedly became a reality in 1965, was not a new one. It had been floating about for eighty years. This essay, written to mark the first ten years of the Secretariat, attempts to put the history and work of the Secretariat into some historical perspective.

WHEN THE PRIME Minister of Australia, Alfred Deakin, reached Colombo on his way to London to attend the Imperial Conference of 1907 he was handed a sheaf of papers from the Colonial Office. He was annoyed; they were the first papers about the meeting he had seen and now no time was left for him to respond with his own ideas. It seemed to him that he was going to a meeting for which there had been almost no preparation. Deakin had been lucky; other Prime Ministers did not receive their papers until they landed in Britain.

The responsibility for this preparation lay with an overstretched Colonial Office, where just two members of the staff worked on the agenda in their spare time. To be fair to them, governments had been slow to submit ideas. The Colonial Secretary, Lord Elgin, had had to nudge New Zealand, and one or two had not answered at all. The British Press, as well as Deakin, was displeased with the situation. *The Times* and *The Morning Post* said that the answer lay in the formation of a special secretariat.

Ever since 1887 feelings had been strong in the Dominions that they should be rid of the Colonial Office. Not unnaturally, now that they were self-governing they did not see why the British Government should still deal with them as though they were colonies. Deakin, a visionary in Commonwealth matters, felt the time had come to change the situation. At the 1907 meeting he proposed to his fellow Prime Ministers of Canada, Newfoundland, New Zealand and South Africa, and to Lord Elgin, in the chair, that a Secretariat should be set up independent of the Colonial Office, supervised by the British Prime Minister and under another British Minister.*

Deakin wanted a Secretariat consisting of people new to public life selected because of their knowledge of the Dominions. The British did not like the idea of a body working outside the Colonial Office, and the Canadian Prime Minister, Sir Wilfrid Laurier, was firmly opposed on the grounds that it might endanger Canadian self-government. Sir Henry Campbell-Bannerman said it would be impossible for the British Prime Minister to supervise the new institution. He did not, however, mind becoming President of the Imperial Conference, and this was agreed.

In the end a compromise was worked out: a Dominions Division

---

* More detailed reference to the beginnings of the secretariat idea are to be found in *The Colonial and Imperial Conferences 1887–1911*, by John Edward Kendle. Longmans. 1967.

14

would be set up in the Colonial Office to prepare further conferences in advance, to serve them when they met and to follow up the resolutions. The Secretariat would not, however, be allowed to correspond with Commonwealth governments directly or through High Commissions. Thus Elgin was left with a complete say in the matter. Deakin was fed up and so was the London Press. L. S. Amery wrote an article in disagreement.

The disappointment turned out to be justified. All that happened was that a Junior Assistant Under-Secretary called Hartmann Just and two clerks were told that from 1 December 1907, they would perform the duties of the Dominions Division in addition to their normal work. They were given no extra accommodation, no extra pay and no secretary. Not surprisingly, nothing happened and when MPs began to ask questions in the House the Parliamentary Under-Secretary for the Colonies, Colonel Jack Seely, gave evasive answers and said that the Secretariat was anyway 'simply a clearing house of information for the Empire'. Eighteen months after the Secretariat came into being only Just seems to have done any work on it. And when the 1911 conference came along the same lack of preparation again manifested itself.

Deakin, now in opposition, developed his original theme when he said in the Australian Parliament on 25 November 1910, that there should be a Secretariat 'in which there shall be Australian officers to represent Australia and other officers to represent the other Dominions'. His idea was 'to reach a common foreign policy by agreement'.

The Colonial Office Secretariat developed no further, and in 1917 it faded out when Sir Maurice Hankey became secretary of the Imperial War Conference. Under him there began a joint Commonwealth Secretariat for the Imperial War Cabinet and this was revived at each meeting of the Imperial Conference from 1921 onwards. Hankey was called 'Secretary-General to the British Empire Delegation'. H. Duncan Hall* writes: 'From 1917 to the Second World War, he was in effect the Secretary-General of the Commonwealth.'

In the 1920s the Australian Prime Minister, S. M. Bruce, supported by the New Zealand Prime Minister, Joseph Gordon Coates, again pressed for a separate Secretariat, but Canada remained hostile to the idea and again nothing came of it. After

---

* *Commonwealth*: A History of the British Commonwealth of Nations. Van Nostrand Reinhold Co.

World War II, with the creation of the Office of Commonwealth Relations, as it was at first called, out of the Dominions Office the exchange of views and information between Commonwealth countries began to develop on a better arranged basis. By the end of the 1950s a substantial organization had been built. Even so, voices continued to favour some independent machinery and one of them was again Australian—the Prime Minister, Robert Menzies.

Later, in the early 1960s, Prime Ministers of the newly independent countries began to come up with complaints that were similar to those of their forerunners half a century earlier. Dr Eric Williams of Trinidad was one who expressed himself as horrified by the casual, almost amateur nature of Prime Ministers' Meetings.

In the end, as the pace of nationalism quickened, the setting up of a Secretariat independent of Whitehall became essential if the Commonwealth was to survive. At the Prime Ministers' Meeting of 1956 the Commonwealth consisted of only eight countries and in 1960 there were still only eleven, but by 1964, at Marlborough House, eighteen sat at the table and a year later twenty-one. It was not to be expected that these countries would be satisfied for long with an arrangement that left in British hands the machinery through which member countries conducted Commonwealth business. By 1964 charges were being made by the newer members that Britain was manipulating the Commonwealth to its own ends—even that Britain was trying to time Commonwealth conferences and adapt agenda to suit the domestic political situation, particularly in relation to the Rhodesian problem. Earlier Canadian arguments had been that a Secretariat would detract from self-government; now the case was reversed.

President Kwame Nkrumah of Ghana proposed the setting up of a Secretariat at the Prime Ministers' Meeting of 1964. Support came from Williams, President Obote of Uganda and President Kenyatta of Kenya and the details were worked out by officials in January 1965. The Commonwealth conference of June that year set up the Secretariat and chose the Canadian diplomat, Arnold Smith as its first Secretary-General.

Sir Alec Douglas-Home, then British Prime Minister, presided over the 1965 meeting and, whatever some Whitehall officials may have thought of the idea, he supported it. Canada was now wholeheartedly in favour, but Australia, represented by Sir Robert Menzies, had cooled. Publicly Sir Robert welcomed the development, but by now he was feeling less sanguine about the way in which the new Commonwealth was developing. The appointment of a Canadian as Secretary-General was not welcome in Canberra and rankled for years.

Much discussion at the 1965 conference centred on the powers which the Secretariat were to be given. The older members of the Commonwealth were particularly anxious that it should not be able in any way to act independently. British officials really wanted it to remain purely a sorting house for information and communication between member countries—the 'clearing house for the Empire' concept of 1907.

The agreed Memorandum on the Secretariat was restrictive and vague and reflected nervousness about the new body. It pointed out that 'The Commonwealth . . . does not encroach on the sovereignty of individual Members' and therefore 'there would be disadvantages in establishing too formal procedures and institutions . . . its staff and functions should be left to expand pragmatically in the light of experience . . .' The Memorandum went on to say that '. . . provided that it begins modestly and remains careful not to trespass on the independence and sovereignty of the Member Governments whose servant it will be, it will be possible for it to grow in the spirit of the Commonwealth association itself'. The one firm and bald warning was this sentence: 'The Secretariat should not arrogate to itself executive functions.'

Mr Smith retired in 1975 after two five-year terms as Secretary-General. This tough, resilient and amiable diplomat inevitably had many critics over the years, but his persistent faith in the Commonwealth idea in sometimes appallingly difficult circumstances coupled with adroit diplomatic skills showed that Commonwealth Governments had made a wise choice. Indeed, any assessment of the work of the Secretariat, which now employs about 300 people from twenty-five countries, must largely be an assessment of the achievement of this one man. Many able diplomats and technical experts assisted him and the contribution of several was immense, but few covered anywhere near the full span of his service. Mr Smith was the dominant and constant Secretariat figure at all the main Commonwealth conferences and in all the main negotiations.

The work of the Secretariat falls under two broad headings: diplomacy and functional co-operation. Each has been dependent on the other, but of the two the diplomatic effort has remained the more vital. To this day the yield from Commonwealth membership in the non-political fields is not by itself sufficiently important to override political considerations. It does not amount to enough ultimately to keep a country in the Commonwealth, though it certainly weighs as a crucial factor.

Much of the diplomacy has been secret; to this extent the lack of public and Press interest in the Secretariat's work, a marked feature of its history to date, has been an asset. The general malaise about the Commonwealth as an association meant a low rate of curiosity about the activities of the Secretary-General and his officials. Their comings and goings often attracted little or no attention, particularly in Britain. The diplomatic achievement is thus much greater than it has appeared to be.

In the first decade there was no single spectacular coup; most of the work was preventive, heading off potential dangers and minimizing others. Most crucial was the success in convincing governments that the Commonwealth was not an extension of the British Empire or a neo-colonial device to continue British influence and interest, but an intricate relationship between thirty-six countries existing for the benefit of each—what Jawaharlal Nehru once called 'independence plus'. Member countries no longer feel that a bilateral quarrel with Britain calls into question its continued membership of the Commonwealth. The Commonwealth is not now seen as a diplomatic liability, but is respected as a genuine international association, membership of which is consistent with independence. The concept of the Commonwealth has acquired credibility.

International acceptance of the Commonwealth in its new form was accelerated by the very problem that dogged it throughout Mr Smith's ten years and more than once almost brought it crashing down—Southern Africa. From the outset Rhodesia was a main preoccupation for the Secretariat; Arnold Smith's task was to try to convince the African leaders that a quarrel with Britain was not a quarrel with the Commonwealth. In doing this he ran the risk of suspicion that he was doing Britain's job. In fact, the British suspected him of showing too much sympathy to the Africans and relations between the Secretariat and Whitehall over this issue often became strained.

The main task was to prevent any country leaving the Commonwealth, for the departure of one would have started a chain reaction. Only by tireless effort involving frequent trips to Africa did Mr Smith and his officials manage to hold the line. In December 1965 Ghana and Tanzania followed the recommendation

18

of the Organization of African Unity that all African countries should break off diplomatic relations with Britain. But neither country left the Commonwealth and for the two-and-a-half years until relations were restored in 1968 President Nyerere of Tanzania kept his country in the Commonwealth, remaining in close contact with the Secretariat, demonstrating practically the point that the Commonwealth was no longer to be viewed as a form of special relationship with Britain. The Secretariat had come into being in the nick of time. Without its existence and with Commonwealth affairs being handled by Whitehall, it is doubtful that Tanzania could have remained in the Commonwealth.

Five years later in July 1970 the threat of withdrawal from the Commonwealth arose as seriously as before when the new British Conservative Government announced that Commonwealth countries were to be consulted about the British intention to sell arms to South Africa. Again the Secretariat counselled caution on all sides. In early October the Tanzanian Cabinet decided (but did not announce) that it would leave the Commonwealth the moment the British formally announced that they would sell arms.

Mr Smith had been warning the British Government for weeks of the danger and had argued that if one country left the Commonwealth others would follow. By now the British were making hard calculations about just how many countries would actually leave; Mr Smith told them that it would not just be a case of two or three quitting but of all the African countries and probably many others besides. President Nyerere flew to Britain for talks with Mr Edward Heath at Chequers and went away in despair. President Kaunda of Zambia headed an OAU delegation to London and had an unhappy experience with Mr Heath over dinner at No 10.

While Mr Smith was holding the African countries at bay he was pressing the British Prime Minister not to act. He finally wrote a special appeal to Mr Heath. The combination of pressures— by this time Sir Alec Douglas-Home, the Foreign and Commonwealth Secretary, had begun to have doubts about the whole exercise—prevented the announcement being made before Heads of Government assembled in Singapore for their January meeting.

The stormy conference ended with the device of the Indian Ocean Study Group which was stillborn because of the British statement a few weeks later that it intended to sell seven Wasp helicopters to South Africa. But now the heat had gone out of the matter; no other arms were sold.*

The Commonwealth had won—an achievement that gained little public recognition, largely because the outcome was blurred over a period; the British never clearly stated that they had decided not to sell more than the helicopters.† In all probability there was private agreement between South Africa and Britain not to pursue further deals.

The Rhodesian and South African arms situations are the most widely known examples of Commonwealth Secretariat diplomacy; a third major effort was at the time of the Nigerian civil war. Months of secret meetings in London and Nigeria marked the Secretariat's efforts to bring about a ceasefire in the civil war and these culminated in bringing together the Nigerian Federal and Biafran delegations in Kampala, Uganda, under President Obote's chairmanship.

Because the talks broke down this piece of diplomacy is seen as a failure, but such an assessment does not take into account the fact that in the bringing of the parties round the table, the internal affairs of an African country were being put under international scrutiny. To this day no other internal situation in independent black Africa has been subjected to such outside mediation. Not even the OAU has broken through this barrier.

The loss of Pakistan was a blow. President Bhutto had invited Mr Smith to Islamabad for talks, but barely two hours before he arrived the British Government ineptly timed the delivery of a Note to Pakistan saying that it had decided to recognize Bangladesh. Before Mr Smith could see Mr Bhutto, Pakistan radio had announced the country's withdrawal from the Commonwealth. Whether Mr Smith might have persuaded the President to change his mind is doubtful, but delay by Whitehall might have helped.

The other side of the Bangladesh story is one of great success. The Secretariat was swift to offer technical aid (Mr Smith led a

* The helicopters were long in delivery and finally, because of the change of government in 1974, the last of the seven was never sent.

† Another reason is that the African governments deliberately, and wisely, showed no public elation. Even Commonwealth observers have been slow to recognize the measure of the African victory on this issue. Professor J. D. B. Miller, in his *Survey of Commonwealth Affairs* (Oxford University Press), argues (p. 165) that African influence in the Commonwealth had by 1970 declined and that 'there was a failure to prevent the sale to South Africa of arms'. The opposite is the case.

20

strong Marlborough House team to Dacca) and Commonwealth governments were persuaded to accept Bangladesh as a Commonwealth member before that country had been accepted into the UN or any other international body. Many Commonwealth governments required careful coercion, since they were not ready to give Bangladesh diplomatic recognition. In traditionally informal Commonwealth style some—Nigeria was one—allowed Bangladesh to join the Commonwealth before they actually recognized the country's existence.

In 1968 the Secretariat became involved in a diplomatic effort brought about by the threatened breakdown of several co-operative efforts between Commonwealth Caribbean countries. The jointly-run University of the West Indies was in danger of being split up because the Jamaican Government was concerned by, among other things, radical student uprisings in Kingston. They complained that they found themselves in the position of not being able to control events in their own country. There were also difficulties in the formation of the Caribbean Development Bank and problems in achieving greater airline co-operation. Trinidad wanted Barbados and Jamaica to join British West Indies Airways. On the University and the Bank the Secretariat was able to prevent and heal the splits. On BWIA it had to admit failure. Jamaica went ahead with its own airline.

A more recent, perhaps crucial, piece of personal diplomacy was achieved by Mr Smith when he met Samora Machel and other leaders of the Mozambique liberation movement, Frelimo, during his visit to Dar es Salaam for the 1974 Saba Saba celebrations. At that time, following a preliminary meeting between the Portuguese Government and Frelimo in Lusaka, independence talks were hanging fire and the Africans were still not convinced that the Portuguese genuinely wanted to confer full independence anyway. Frelimo were becoming impatient. They asked Mr Smith to tell the Portuguese Government that if Lisbon did not get in touch with them by 20 July they would conclude that Portugal was not interested in proceeding with independence for Mozambique. On his return Mr Smith conveyed the message to the Portuguese Foreign Minister, Mario Soares, and soon afterwards Portuguese contact with Frelimo was resumed.

At one time the then President, General Spinola, was talking in terms of a 'Lusitanian commonwealth' solution as if it were an alternative to full independence. The Secretariat was not slow to point out to Lisbon that Commonwealth countries had full independence and that a commonwealth solution could not be an alternative.

In the end the Commonwealth Secretariat played no active role in the agreement reached between the forty-six African, Caribbean and Pacific (ACP) group of countries and the European Economic Community which culminated in the Lomé Convention signed in February 1975, though at a much earlier stage it was instrumental in helping Commonwealth countries individually and collectively to negotiate successfully. Apart from preparing for member countries studies of their individual situation *vis-à-vis* the EEC, the Secretariat mounted two conferences of officials (April and July 1972) at which the Secretary-General urged Commonwealth countries to stand together in negotiation at Brussels; only by doing so would developing countries be able to exert fully their bargaining power. Secretariat attempts to mount further meetings of Commonwealth officials, including one at ministerial level, failed. It is questionable whether the Secretariat might have continued to play a role; the initiative moved to the OAU which then, led by Nigeria, brought the other Caribbean and Pacific countries together.

But the unity which the Secretariat had advocated was totally achieved. The forty-six stuck together and the result was Lomé. Although the French had not liked the Marlborough House activity (at one time Mr Smith came under heavy fire in the French Press), the Secretariat had not preached unity to the developing countries—and a firm recommendation against accepting the idea of reverse preferences—because of any hostility to the EEC; Mr Smith had done so believing that the right link between Commonwealth countries and Europe would be beneficial to both. As Secretary-General he never took the line that the EEC and the Commonwealth were incompatible; on the contrary, he favoured British membership of the Community and did not see it as inimical to the Commonwealth interest. It proved a diplomatically brave and wise stance.

The second side of the Secretariat's work—the long, painstaking building of functional co-operation—is a heartening story. Behind the stormy political scene in the late 1960s the areas of co-operation readily grew. The Nairobi conference of senior economic planners in 1967 was one turning point; from it sprang the Commonwealth Fund for Technical Co-operation, an aid scheme

22

unique in character that has mushroomed recently. From the valuable series of seminars on Youth and Development held in several Commonwealth capitals came the Commonwealth Youth Programme. From meetings of Cabinet Secretaries and other senior Commonwealth officials came the establishment of a programme to provide senior public servants with opportunities for study and the exchange of experience. From a conference on Food and Rural Development in 1975 came the formation of a new Food Production and Rural Development Division within the Secretariat to provide financial help in rural development.

The range of work being performed by the Secretariat is ever-widening: the study of subjects such as the role of multinational corporations, the problems of pluralism in island communities, and the place of universities in national development; book development; the training of legislative draughtsmen and financial journalists; studies aimed at boosting exports for developing countries; even how to make the teaching of mathematics more interesting. Regional Secretariats have been established. A Regional Health Bureau for East, Central and Southern Africa has been set up in Arusha, Tanzania, and a West African Bureau is situated in Lagos. The Secretariat has permanent representatives now in the Caribbean, Papua New Guinea and Geneva and youth centres in Chandigarh, India, Georgetown, Guyana, and Lusaka, Zambia.

The development of this multi-faceted Commonwealth is largely due to the energy and drive shown at Marlborough House. Before 1965 few officials in the Commonwealth Relations Office were 'thinking Commonwealth'. This was not necessarily their fault; the CRO was a ministry of the British Government and it was natural that the British interest should come first in its thinking and influence decisions. The new Commonwealth could not be organized in this way.

Since 1965 a steadily increasing international band of civil servants have been devoting all their thoughts and energies to ways of making the Commonwealth work as an association. They have achieved results, sometimes in the most frustrating circumstances and occasionally without being sure that at the end of the day there would be a Commonwealth at all.

Any assessment of the work at the Secretariat's first decade must take into account the political turbulence of at least half that period. In the first few months of the Secretariat's existence war broke out between India and Pakistan; Ian Smith declared UDI; the Nigerian Prime Minister was assassinated within hours of chairing the first Commonwealth conference held outside London and the first to be organized by the Secretariat; and President Nkrumah (a co-founder of the Secretariat) was toppled. Today's Commonwealth is calm by comparison.

It was just as well that the founding fathers in 1965 gave the Secretariat vague terms of reference. Arnold Smith exploited his situation to the full and was often daring in his interpretations. Those who wanted the Secretariat to be a postbox were to be disappointed; it has become far from that. Under the wrong Secretary-General the story might have been different.

It was also particularly fortunate that the first Secretary-General was from one of the largest Commonwealth countries. A man from a small country would not have succeeded in overcoming the pressures and pinpricks that in the early days came from the direction of Whitehall.

Mr Smith had behind him from the outset the firm support of Lester Pearson, the Canadian Prime Minister from 1963 to 1968. The two were personally close and Pearson was a firm believer in the modern Commonwealth. The Canadian role in the Secretariat's activity throughout has been of deep importance.

The Secretariat has grown in size year by year and the danger of over-bureaucratization has not to be overlooked. So far it has managed to maintain an informality and a flexibility that other international organizations have lacked. Early arguments against any such institution as a Secretariat were based on the fact that the Commonwealth should have no formal administrative machinery. They were wrong arguments because today's Commonwealth is based not on emotional attachments but on hard-headed common sense arrangements between states.

Mr Smith's style suited the times and on his retirement in 1975 he handed over a going concern; the position of Secretary-General had been established and the status of the Secretariat was now respected throughout the Commonwealth and outside.

Deakin, more than half a century ahead of his time, would be pleased at the way it has all turned out.

CHAPTER THREE
London 1969: False Dawn

At the two traumatic Heads of Government conferences held in 1966—the first in Lagos, Nigeria, in January and the second in London in September—Commonwealth fortunes reached a low ebb, mainly because of deep differences between Britain and the new African countries over the way to handle rebellious Rhodesia.

A gap of nearly two and a half years followed before Commonwealth leaders met again, during the whole of which Rhodesia continued to dominate and agitate Commonwealth political affairs.

From the end of the Sixties fundamental changes began to take place in the Commonwealth relationship, particularly between the developing member-countries and the former metropolitan power, Britain.

The next four chapters trace the mood before and after the four summit conferences which really changed the face of the Commonwealth—starting with the one held in London in January 7-15 1969. This meeting, so much more cordial than those held in 1966, nonetheless turned out to be something of a false Commonwealth dawn, as this first report, written in December 1968 shows . . .

THE MEETING OF Commonwealth Heads of Government in London holds promise of being more fruitful than any held since 1961, the year South Africa withdrew. Each of the five subsequent meetings tended to be dominated by a single problem: in 1962 Britain's application to join the Common Market; in 1964, 1965 and September 1966 Rhodesia (the first 1966 meeting in Lagos was, of course, called specifically to discuss Rhodesia). In these seven years Commonwealth membership has almost doubled in size (in 1961 only 13 countries were represented) and now we see the association in just about its full plumage.

The turnout of Presidents and Prime Ministers for a Heads of Government conference is unlikely ever again to be 100 per cent—if only because by the law of averages political or physical ailments are bound to prevent a number of leaders from attending. All the same, the January meeting looks like being an impressive affair; probably not since the Khrushchev shoe-banging meeting at the UN General Assembly in 1961 will the world have seen such a star-studded assembly of world leaders. There have been many moments in the last few years when not even the most incurable Commonwealth enthusiast could conceive the possibility of such a gathering taking place, and certainly it is little short of astonishing that the Commonwealth has survived Rhodesia. If ever a problem should have shattered the Commonwealth into slivers it was Rhodesia. Yet it did not.

The genesis of the 1969 conference was a pressure movement of opinion in some Commonwealth capitals last year that the Commonwealth must try to get off the Rhodesia hook; that somehow ways must be found of holding a conference to discuss basic issues, such as the whole philosophy of the association, without its being preoccupied with Rhodesia. Support was found among governments for such a meeting, but, as always, the seed was slow to germinate. Eventually it was agreed that Rhodesia or not, there certainly should be a Commonwealth conference in 1968.

The timing of conferences has always been erratic, although Prime Ministers did once agree to meet every year. In 1965-6 there were three meetings, yet in the period 1957-60 there were only two. Sounding out twenty-eight governments is no fast process, unless it is on a matter of dramatic urgency. The exercise takes many weeks. Nor is it now just a question of fixing the date of a Heads of Government meeting; the venue also is a matter for discussion. Since the precedent of Lagos, 1966, Britain is no longer the auto-

26

matic choice.

From the outset there was a strong feeling in favour of having the conference outside Britain. A contention of some of the newer members is that during the two previous conferences in London Britain still tried to run the Commonwealth her way. In 1965 the nimble British footwork that produced the Vietnam peace mission left a nasty taste in many mouths; and again in September 1966 Mr Wilson seemed to be trying to manoeuvre the Commonwealth to his own domestic political advantages. At the turn of this year President Nyerere and President Kaunda remained at loggerheads with Mr Wilson and it looked likely that neither would attend a conference if it were held in Britain.

Eyes therefore switched to Canada and to its internationalist Prime Minister, Lester Pearson. Ottawa seemed the perfect answer. The crowning achievement of a great diplomatic career, argued some of his friends, could be chairmanship of this conference. No doubt the idea appealed to Pearson, but he was deeply immersed in the problem of his withdrawal from political life and how he might effect a transfer of leadership that would keep the Liberal Party in power. Pearson could not be budged. Suddenly he gave a firm date for his resignation as Prime Minister—months before the projected conference—and Ottawa as a site was out. When Pierre Trudeau took over neither he nor his Conservative Party opponent, Robert Stanfield—whichever was in power when the time came—would commit himself as host and Ottawa as a possible venue.

For a long while it was a case of a conference in search of a meeting place. The more people looked around the twenty-eight capitals, the more difficult it seemed: Africa was out because there was a need for 'neutral' ground in the context of Rhodesia; Rawalpindi seemed out because President Ayub was for a time in bad health; Delhi had just been host to a huge UNCTAD conference. There seemed a snag to every place. The Caribbean was favoured and Barbados was offered; Trinidad and Barbados, it was suggested, could be joint hosts and Dr Eric Williams of Trinidad, as senior Caribbean Prime Minister, would take the chair. While all this was going on the British Government, which had earlier accepted Ottawa, started pressing for the conference to be held in London. Hitherto, it had not seemed anxious to be host; now that view had changed.

Some governments were distinctly hostile to this idea. Zambia wanted Barbados; Tanzania did not see how it could attend if

27

diplomatic relations with Britain remained ruptured. Malawi did not want a conference at all. India was aloof. Then someone suddenly realized that 7 October—the proposed date—was the week of the Conservative Party conference. Was Mr Wilson up to his old tricks again, trying to use the conference to steal the headlines from Mr Heath? One President at least was annoyed and said that, though he wanted to attend a Commonwealth conference, he did not intend to be used in a game of British politics. The weeks wore on inconclusively. It began to look as if October might produce a poor muster. The British Government were a little peeved and Mr Wilson even showed his impatience in a House of Commons reply:

> I am disappointed that the date of the conference is as late as it is . . . We should have preferred it to have been held this autumn.*

Finally, it was agreed to speed a decision by calling a meeting of High Commissioners at the Secretariat. Now Tanzania was back in relations with Britain and President Kaunda was on better terms with Mr Wilson. London was more popular and January seemed a better time for everyone.

It still seems unfortunate that the conference is once more in London, though it is true an acceptable meeting ground is not easy to find—and not only for political or diplomatic reasons. Barbados has obvious snags as a communications centre; twenty-eight Heads of Government all wanting to keep in touch with their capitals would strain the resources of tiny Bridgetown. London is still a popular choice even with the new members; Botswana, for example, favoured London all along.

What of the prospects? The three months' delay may in the end prove to have been a blessed gift. This 1969 conference requires, if nothing else, to be a thoughtful one. The Commonwealth, having now arrived at its approximate permanent composition and having walked through the Valley of the Shadow of Death, has reached the point where it needs to take a cool look at itself. If the 1969 conference can manage—and it is a big if—to look beyond immediate political preoccupations and spend considerable time debating the aims and objects of the association and what shape the Commonwealth should take in the next decade (indeed whether governments want a Commonwealth at all), then much could be achieved. This can only happen if:

* *Hansard*, July 23, 1968.

28

1. There is a good muster of Prime Ministers and Presidents. Experience has shown that the quality of debate is markedly higher when the top men are there. Only then does discussion reach out beyond bread-and-butter politics.

2. Some distracting issue does not blow up just before the conference. One difficulty in the past has been that time has tended to be spent on a subject which happens to be making the headlines at the particular moment of the meeting. For example, had the conference been sitting last August, the Czech situation* might have been debated at length under the traditional heading 'Review of International Affairs'. A month later the Czech issue had receded, and a conference then might have given the subject scant attention. When a Heads of Government conference is held only every two or three years and the real need is to look at the state of the Commonwealth itself, such distractions can neutralize the conference's long-term effect.

African affairs are still a danger: the three months' delay may mean the diminution of Nigeria† as a major issue; so far as Rhodesia is concerned, forecasts are dangerous. Rhodesia no longer generates the intense political heat it did two years ago, but it would be surprising if Mr Smith was not thinking up a move that will cause Britain maximum embarrassment just before the conference. Smith's timing is always clever; hangings of Africans and false peace overtures are two of several weapons at his disposal.

It is in Smith's interest to do all possible damage and disrupt the Commonwealth. Nothing will be more harmful to the conference in January than more long wrangles over Rhodesia—and he knows that. Certainly the climate around the Commonwealth since the last meeting—and particularly in the last few months—has changed, but this is not to say that almost all the African and Asian countries feel any differently on the principles of the issue; they are as firm as ever. There has simply been an acceptance that the problem is a much longer-term one than they once thought, and that the turmoil of southern Africa will have to be lived with.

Even in Africa itself attitudes have changed; in some places the faces have changed. Siaka Stevens, of Sierra Leone, is something apart from the fire-eating Albert Margai,‡ Ankrah§ sees it quite differently from Nkrumah, Gowon is preoccupied, Banda some-

* The rebellion in Prague put down by Russian troops.

† The civil war was then raging.

‡ Margai had been particularly militant against Britain at the 1966 meetings. He lost power in 1967 and is now living in exile in Britain.

§ Major-General Ankrah headed the new military government of Ghana.

29

times seems to sympathize with Smith, Sir Seretse Khama (Botswana), Chief Leabua Jonathan (Lesotho) and Prince Makhosini Dlamini (Swaziland) are not in favour of a lot of noise. Presidents Nyerere and Kaunda reluctantly realize that Britain is going to maintain her lame-duck attitudes and that there is a great deal else to be discussed about the Commonwealth.

Indeed, it is Nyerere who is showing more concern than almost anyone else about making the Commonwealth a really valuable world organization. By remaining in the Commonwealth while out of diplomatic relations with Britain he demonstrated to everyone that the Commonwealth was a relationship between Tanzania and twenty-six other nations apart from Britain. It was a most heartening development, and if this message could be put across to a number of other member-countries the outlook for the Commonwealth would be bright indeed.

In particular does this apply to India and Australia—currently the 'indifferents' on the Commonwealth map. There is an almost total lack of enthusiasm for the Commonwealth in Delhi and Canberra, and it is alarming (and at the same time perhaps comforting in that they are not part of a *bloc*) that one country is of the so-called old Commonwealth and the other of the New—the founder of the New Commonwealth, in fact. In both cases disenchantment with the Commonwealth has come about because of disenchantment with Britain. Neither country sees the Commonwealth as much more than a relationship with Britain and because that relationship is bad the Commonwealth is in disfavour. Mrs Gandhi does not see the Commonwealth as more than a debating shop and her views have undoubtedly been influenced by Mr Wilson's famous Kashmir statement* and his continued failure to carry out promises to visit India.* Repeated cries for India's withdrawal from the Commonwealth in Parliament and the press are almost invariably based on the current state of relations between India and Britain.

It is particularly sad that India as the largest member-state and the first of the 'new' ones cannot apparently recognize that she occupies the key position in the Commonwealth. If she really set her mind to it she could exert enormous influence, taking initiatives and showing a real lead. It is all there for the taking; tailor-made for her. No Indian Prime Minister has attended a Heads of Government conference since Lal Bahadur Shastri in 1965, and it will be a

* The statement had upset the Indian Government.

30

severe shock if Mrs Gandhi does not come to London in January.

In the case of Australia, the general abrasiveness in relations between Britain and Australia is rubbing off on the Commonwealth all the time. Rhodesia has not helped; Australians and white Rhodesians are made of similar settler stuff and Australians are thus not much 'in sympathy with the African cause. They continuously contend now that their first interest is in Asia, yet they do not seem to see that their Commonwealth relationships in Asia are something that can be built on and developed. Mrs Gandhi visited Australia earlier this year; it would be interesting to know whether the word 'Commonwealth' ever crossed the lips of either of them during the visit, although their relationships are certainly conditioned by the many factors they share in common through the Commonwealth connection. However, Mr Gorton will undoubtedly attend the conference in London. It will be a new experience for him* and perhaps he will be impressed by what he sees.

The conference, therefore, barring accidents, is likely to take stock of the Commonwealth and there is no more valuable thing it can do. It will be able to look back at an impressive amount of work achieved since the last Heads of Government conference—major conferences on health (Kampala), education (Lagos), aid and planning (Nairobi), tourism (Valletta)—not to mention smaller or more regular groups such as the Telecommunications council, the Commonwealth Parliamentary Association, Auditors-General, Finance Ministers, Forestry Officials and the expanding work of such bodies as the Commonwealth Foundation.

It seems a fair bet that immigration will be a subject for discussion. The subject is spiky, but an important one to tackle, if only perhaps to show that it is not such a menace as everyone seems to think. The problem of publicizing the Commonwealth now that Britain has largely—and rightly—given up the job of doing it herself is likely to loom large. It is plain that Commonwealth booklets, fact sheets and so forth should be produced by the Commonwealth as a body (and by this is meant under the auspices of the Secretariat) and not only by one of its member-countries. One reason why the Commonwealth gets a poor press is that few people have in their minds a complete picture of activity; they know only about the workings of one or more component parts. An in-

---

* He had become Prime Minister in 1968 after Harold Holt was drowned. He was replaced in 1971 by William McMahon.

formation division of the Secretariat is thus essential.

There will be an attempt to give a new push to many of the ideas accepted by the education, medical and planning conferences. Commonwealth education co-operation has been outstandingly fruitful and the plans for specialist conferences such as on Curriculum Development, Education in Rural Areas, the Role of New Media in Education and the Humanities and Social Sciences will no doubt be given the blessing of the Heads of Government. Then the conference will take a look at the way regional co-operation is developing in the Commonwealth. In East Africa, in the Caribbean and in south-East Asia groupings, mainly of Commonwealth countries, have developed fast and successfully. It could be fruitful for the London conference to look into how the Commonwealth as a whole is affected by these regional developments.

The attitude of Britain at the Commonwealth conference will be closely watched. Has Whitehall finally grasped the new situation? If only because some Commonwealth countries still base their attitude to the Commonwealth on their attitude to Britain it will be more important than ever that Mr Wilson as host and chairman does not try to use the conference to further his own domestic political image. The temptation will be there, more especially because he has hit hard times at Westminster.

One of the disappointments of the Labour Government has been the discovery that its leader and many of its members have a more old-fashioned and paternalistic attitude towards the developing countries than Sir Alec Douglas-Home and some Tory ministers. Part of the original Labour platform was to further the development of Commonwealth ideas, but these ideas were soon seen to be desperately out of date and out of touch. Mr Wilson himself did not know Africa or Asia and, in office, he did not show signs of wanting to know much except where it was essential to him politically, as in the case of Rhodesia. Travel around the Commonwealth for him obviously had low priority. The visit to India was not made;* a visit to Australia only made to attend Holt's funeral; a visit to Canada simply, one suspects, because Ottawa lay on the way home from Washington. Perhaps Mr Wilson saw no votes in visits to Asia and Africa. Mr Macmillan saw things differently; he constantly travelled about the Commonwealth and gained inter-

---

* Mr Wilson twice told Mrs Gandhi he would visit India, but in the end during more than eight years as Prime Minister he never did.

national and national prestige in doing so.

A lack of enthusiasm in the Commonwealth seemed to grip much of Whitehall, to which was added no great liking by some officials—though not by all—for the Commonwealth Secretariat. It was inevitable that the Secretariat, whose task it was to take functions away from Whitehall, would meet some opposition, and it was equally inevitable that relations would later settle down and improve. This is now happening. Ironically, the best team at the Commonwealth Office for years—Mr George Thomson, as Secretary of State, and Sir Morrice James, as Permanent Under-Secretary*—have had only a few months in action together, but they have made their mark, and if a new British attitude to the Commonwealth is beginning to emerge, the credit goes largely to these two men. It remains to be seen whether this new thinking can be carried right through to the new combined Commonwealth and Foreign Office.†

The signs for January, then, are on the whole good. For the first time for years there are indications that imaginative thinking is coming forth from Whitehall. The Prime Minister may well have learnt that the Commonwealth has wider applications than a platform for short-term political ideas (though the pressure for the Heads of Government meeting at Tory Party conference time was a depressing adherence to past form).

By any present-day international standards the conference in January will be remarkable. An organization that can bring together under one roof such a host of major world figures as Lee, Trudeau, Nyerere, Wilson, Mrs Gandhi, Ayub, Makarios, Williams and Gorton must be adjudged a phenomenon. Maybe, as on previous occasions, the conference will be heralded with lukewarm enthusiasm by many commentators and even hostility and negativity by a few. Headlines may not refrain from such labels as 'the make-or-break conference', and I suppose there will be at least one commentator who will predict before it has started that this is the last Heads of Government conference. Yet I sense that we may now be at the end of this period of fashionable disenchantment. There is, for the first time for years, an air of constructiveness at

---

* Mr Thomson, later an EEC Commissioner, held the post for only fourteen months as the last of the line. Sir Morrice James had been High Commissioner in Pakistan. More recently he was High Commissioner in Australia. Both are now peers.

† The two offices were combined on 17 October 1968 and Michael Stewart became the first Secretary of State for Foreign and Commonwealth affairs.

last in a number of countries.

True, it is only as yet 'an air'. But it could be fresh air.

The London conference turned out quite successfully; at the time perhaps it seemed of more significance than it actually was. This was my assessment at the end of the meeting . . .

It still seems too good to be true. Two or three years ago not even the most fervent Commonwealth enthusiast felt confident enough to forecast that twenty-four out of twenty-eight Commonwealth leaders would sit down together in 1969 and hold a thoroughly successful meeting. After September 1966 many observers said that there would never be another Commonwealth Heads of Government conference. Others felt, with good reason, that to try to hold the next meeting in London would unnecessarily court trouble. The chairmanship of Mr Harold Wilson, not wholly popular with many Commonwealth leaders in 1965 and 1966, was questioned.

In the end all these forebodings turned out to be uncalled-for, although the coolness of British Press and television reaction to the January visitors and to the conference generally—in some cases amounting to hostility and cheap rudeness—was something leaders would have been spared in any other Commonwealth capital.

Exactly how successful was the conference? Even before it ended there was a tendency to exult simply because there had been no stand-up rows over Rhodesia, no boycotts, no walkouts. By the end one could almost hear the sighs of relief all down Pall Mall because nothing nasty had happened. That was certainly encouraging, but only negatively so: to fear disaster and then to discover that it has not taken place after all simply brings us back to where we were.

No, the really major achievement of this conference was the marked change of attitude to each other, to the conference and to the Commonwealth that was displayed by just about every delegate to Marlborough House. All twenty-eight came in a mood to listen to one another and to try to understand everyone else's point of view, even though they might (and did) profoundly disagree with it.

Many of the older hands came to the table a little wiser: Mr Wilson now realized that he was handling not a meeting of the British Cabinet but a gathering of men as sovereign as himself, holding views as viable as his own; African leaders, for their part, had seen that their early post-independence tactics of fire and frenzy were now no longer appropriate. Not quite all the bulldog's teeth had been pulled and the bark 'We're independent too' was not to be ignored. New hands came accepting their juniority as new boys of the club. None fired wild broadsides after the manner of Albert Margai, Sierra Leone's former Prime Minister.

Many British commentators were completely thrown by the different atmosphere of the meeting. Some were to be, found wandering around the Press section at Marlborough House asking 'What's gone wrong?' The explosions they expected had not materialized and they were distinctly lost. They had not studied form. The chemistry of the meeting had changed and this they had failed to recognize. Even more importantly, they had failed to relate the change to the work of the chemist's shop: the Commonwealth Secretariat.

Perhaps this is understandable, even something to applaud. True diplomacy should take place unnoticed and here was an example of it. Secretary-General Arnold Smith and his team had worked for more than two years with patience and energy to produce just the kind of Heads of Government gathering that finally emerged. In September 1966 they could see that the next meeting needed to be a carefully planned effort. There was a delicate repair job to be done. The Commonwealth really could not survive many more meetings as divisive as the two 1966 gatherings.

In September 1966 the Secretariat was barely one year old. It had had to organize two Heads of Government meetings in one year (the first was in Lagos in January) and it had been given little time to prepare either. Now there looked like being time. As it turned out, there was plenty. The 1969 meeting was almost a year in the making; the postponement from October 1968 to January gave another valuable three months on top of that.

The Secretariat always saw the crucial importance of a big turnout of the top men; a meeting at which half the delegates were Deputy Premiers or Deputy Presidents or just Cabinet Ministers could never carry the necessary authority. Deputies tended either not to commit themselves at all or else felt the urge to put on a show and overplay their hands.

The British Government, too, (once it had committed itself to a London meeting) worked hard to achieve a high turnout. Particular attention was paid to doubtful starters. Mr Michael Stewart, the Foreign and Commonwealth Secretary, switched his limited charm on Mrs Gandhi when he was in Delhi in December and, when Dr

Banda looked like hesitating, Mr Malcolm MacDonald was des-
patched to Blantyre to stop the President of Malawi from
dithering. (After all, the Doctor was a rare ally on Rhodesia.)*

First prize for the overall achievement of a score of twenty-four
out of twenty-eight must, however, go to the Secretariat. Over
several months it was able to relay all the arguments for and against
between the twenty-eight leaders and to give its own non-partisan
observations.

No one expected, with the big expansion of Commonwealth
membership, that Heads of Government conferences could now
achieve a more than sixty to seventy per cent turnout—if only
because of leaders' possible domestic, political or health preoccupations. In the event the figure was around ninety per cent and
none of the four who stayed away did so because of lack of interest:
President Kenyatta does not fly long distances any more; Major
General Gowon and President Ayub Khan had grave internal problems on their hands, and General Ankrah was adhering to the
Ghana National Liberation Council's rigid adherence to a doctrine
of collective power.

On the other hand, many leaders left urgent domestic affairs in
order to attend: President Kaunda had just emerged from a general
election campaign: Premier Forbes Burnham of Guyana had done
likewise and had also, till the last day, been coping with the
Rupununi uprising;† Mrs Gandhi was engated in crucial mid-term
elections.

It is important to remember that before the Secretariat came into
existence in 1965 the mustering of Heads of Government was
carried out by the British Government. The Secretariat has now
become the diplomatic machine responsible for this exercise and
for the content of Commonwealth dialogue. This is why credit for
the new atmosphere and improved result of the 1969 conference
must largely be attributed to the thorough groundwork—and deft
field-work—of the Commonwealth Secretariat. The difference is
fundamental: there is now a team of international civil servants
whose sole interest is the Commonwealth as a whole, picking up
and developing new ideas that are put forward, preparing papers,

* Malawi, developing a policy of dialogue with South Africa at this time, did not
dissent from British policy on Rhodesia and was out of step with other African
Commonwealth leaders.

† Disturbances by the Amerindians had just taken place in South Guyana.

discovering where the ground is fertile for development and where it is not, probing at problems.

Those who have discussed the Commonwealth in the popular media in Britain have signally failed to recognize this development and therefore the calm and constructiveness of the 1969 conference has made no sense to them at all. If it may be thought that this is putting too much emphasis on the Secretariat's work it must be added that this was by no means the only factor: it was simply the key factor.

The real value of this conference will only emerge over the coming months. On the three crucial issues—Rhodesia, Nigeria and immigration—results on the surface look slim indeed. Yet that may not prove to be the case. The Africans may have appeared to retreat somewhat on their Rhodesian stand but, in fact, they may have found a much better rock in which to stand: the proper testing of opinion of the people of Rhodesia.

The six principles are open to all manner of interpretations; NIBMAR* is a simplification. 'The democratically ascertained wishes of the people,'† however, is an expression that sums up something rather dear and sacred to the British. Anything that goes against 'the wishes of the people' is traditionally disliked in Britain. This is much better ground on which Wilson can argue with his critics against giving in to Smith and it is much better ground on which the Africans can stand and fight Britain (is not this the very principle she is constantly quoting on Gibraltar?).

At Marlborough House the East African leaders Nyerere, Kaunda and Obote profoundly impressed men like Gorton and Holyoake with the calm, coherent intellectual purity of their arguments. Nyerere made a particularly deep impact on the whole conference. Holyoake was said to have declared that the President's opening speech on Rhodesia was the finest he had ever heard anywhere.

It seems possible that the two-day debate on Rhodesia, which one delegate claimed was the best on the subject heard in any international forum since UDI, has left a lasting impression on all the hundred-odd people sitting in that conference room. One comment

* No Independence Before Majority Rule—a principle insisted on by African leaders, only accepted with reluctance by the British.

† Paragraph 31 of the conference communiqué states: 'It was agreed that any settlement must depend for its validity upon the democratically ascertained wishes of the people of Rhodesia as a whole.'

afterwards was that 'The whole thing should have been televised.' (Of course, if it had been televised it would have been a totally different debate.)

No one should be lulled into thinking that Rhodesia is not still an issue which gnaws at the vitals of the Commonwealth. It could still wreck the Commonwealth and there is good reason to believe that Presidents Nyerere and Kaunda made it clear to Mr Wilson privately that their countries would leave the Commonwealth if the *Fearless* proposals* were implemented without hundred per cent evidence that the Africans in Rhodesia had accepted them.

Nigeria was the big disappointment of the conference—not for what did not take place in Marlborough House but for what did not take place in the hotel suites outside. With twelve members of the Organization of African Unity present in London, Biafran representatives at hand and Secretariat machinery available the ingredients for mediation were there. The will for peace, however, was not and attempts to produce any result were still-born. All attempts to get at the problem failed.

Yet even this barren ground could bear fruit. President Nyerere of Tanzania and President Kaunda of Zambia—representing the only two Commonwealth countries which have recognized Biafra—did meet Chief Awolowo.† President Obote, who as host to the Kampala‡ talks, remains deeply interested in the problem, discussed Nigeria with many leaders. Obote, Kaunda and Nyerere are close friends and, the last two having influence with Ojukwu, who can tell what may eventuate from all these contacts in due course—maybe again within the context of the OAU?§

On immigration, the Secretariat has now become involved for the first time. It is asked by those countries concerned about the subject.‖

---

* In October 1968 Wilson had met Smith on board the warship *Fearless*. His proposals fell well short on majority rule. Smith eventually rejected them.

† Awolowo was Vice-Chairman of the Federal Executive Council.

‡ See Chapter Two.

§ In the end the war was fought to a Federal victory.

‖ The seventeen countries which had discussions on migration outside the conference were: Barbados, Botswana, Canada, Ceylon, Cyprus, Guyana, India, Jamaica, Kenya, Malta, Mauritius, New Zealand, Pakistan, Tanzania, Trinidad, Uganda and the UK. Kenya, Uganda, Tanzania withdrew at an early stage.

to examine . . . general principles relating to short and long term movement of people between their countries and to consider the possibility of exploring ways and means of studying this subject on a continuing basis with a view to providing relevant information to those Governments.

The group of countries which held preliminary talks on migration outside the main conference was notable for the inclusion of Canada and New Zealand and the absence of Australia. Australia remains unnecessarily over-sensitive on the migration issue and it would be good to see her joining the group at a later stage. If New Zealand is an interested party, why not Australia?

As on previous occasions, it was in the unnoticed, uncontroversial fields that the conference did a lot of its most useful work. Malta raised the issue of international control of the seabed and leaders heard at first hand about the work that country has put into this problem* and the quite staggering magnitude of it. If, as a result of the conference, the Commonwealth countries act in unison on this crucial issue at the United Nations, that alone would be a justification for this January meeting.

The conference has given the Secretariat much work to do:

1. The extension of the third-party aid scheme started at Nairobi so that students can train in countries more in tune with their eventual jobs. This would ease the brain drain out of developing countries.

2. The study of a Commonwealth information programme.

3. The study of co-operation in the fields of mass communications and education.

4. The setting up of a legal section in the Secretariat.

5. Plans for a conference on legal education.

6. The study of problems of youth.

7. The study of plans for a Commonwealth Book Development Programme to help developing countries to obtain books and journals for education and research.

These items are the also-rans in the Commonwealth conference communiqué and, as such, they received scarcely a mention when the results of the conference were assessed. Yet this is good solid work of value to all the member-countries and a sound result for the conference.

When we add to the above points all the bonuses of personal contact—the reality of twenty-four Heads of Government repeatedly

* For the classic Maltese analysis of this problem, see Arvid Pardo, 'Sovereignty under the Sea', *The Round Table*, No. 232, pages 341-55.

meeting each other over a period of ten days—it seems extra-ordinarily odd and sad that there are some people in Britain who still want to write it all off as a worthless exercise.

Now that the conference has been shown to be a success, it becomes important to look ahead to future conferences and to question some of the procedures. However successful the conference may have been, there is a need for criticism. The British have suggested that the Commonwealth should aim at a conference every eighteen months. The Secretariat was asked by the conference to begin soundings at the end of this year.

With member-countries totalling nearly thirty it could be over-ambitious to try to meet too often. Every two to two-and-a-half years would seem more realistic. If meetings are too frequent countries will acquire the habit of sending deputies; the longer gap would also mean a fair sprinkling of new faces each time that would give an added incentive to attendance in person. It will always be important to keep the attendance at top level, for the reasons already given.

A change of venue is also important. Some capitals would have to be ruled out automatically because of lack of facilities and communications and for security reasons, but it would not be difficult to name half a dozen as highly suitable: New Delhi, Nairobi, Canberra, Ottawa, Wellington, Valletta. Kenya has already offered Nairobi. Delhi would be splendidly appropriate, being the capital of the Commonwealth's largest country, and a conference there would help to rekindle Indian interest in the Commonwealth. For several reasons the next conference should be held east of Suez.

The form of the conference has changed over the years by a process of evolution. As with everything else in the Commonwealth the rules are made up as they go along. It may now be time to question one or two of the traditions. There were, for example, several grumbles this year that too many long set speeches were made (though these were fewer than in previous years) and that not enough time was given for discussion across the table. This was particularly true of the international affairs debate which opened the conference, though here again the debate proved more profitable for all concerned this time because speakers concentrated on telling their colleagues how world problems looked from their particular corner of the world. A new dimension was added to everyone's thinking. (Once again, the Secretariat preparation had helped construct a framework for the speeches.) Perhaps a way can be found to change the pattern, without destroying the content, of this important traditional debate.

Then there was some criticism of the fact that Britain still had two seats at the table while everyone else had one (the second was usually occupied by Mr Stewart). The British claim that this is because the Prime Minister is chairman. The Canadians were surprised that the British had the cheek to stick to this tradition and still more surprised that everyone else let them get away with it.* Britain keeps protesting that she is an equal partner; she still does not always show that she really means it.

An overhaul seems necessary in the press arrangements. Delegations are free to give briefings at any time of the day and national press officers often run hotfoot from the conference room bearing copies of the speech just made by their masters. The debate is secret, and the understanding is that the contents of speeches can only be made public if the speaker ordains it.

Press briefings and news handouts of speeches are comparatively new to Commonwealth Heads of Government conferences. The great merit of these conferences is their secrecy and the fact that no votes are taken, no resolutions moved. These characteristics make the meetings unlike any other international gatherings. There is a case for going backwards a little—namely, for the distribution of speeches to be stopped and for delegations to desist from giving their own briefings. The Secretariat briefings should be enough.

If the meeting is to be secret it is always going to be difficult to prevent leaks and to prevent inaccurate stories appearing. Charges of news management are always going to be made. If, however, the rules of the game are more powerfully put (most of the journalists at Marlborough House had not even grasped the fact that there are no resolutions and votes) then the sympathy of the Press might to a certain extent be won over.

Finally, the shape of the conference. Does it last too long? Some suggestions were made in January that a week should be long enough, and that there were too many diplomatic receptions. Perhaps. But the main concern of the organizer should be that there is plenty of time for all the leaders to meet informally. The more world leaders are thrown together to chat among themselves the better.

---

* Britain now has only one seat like everyone else.

The excursions to Chequers and Dorneywood* may be valuable to the British Government, but would it not have been far better if the twenty-eight had gone off together for an informal weekend and talked among themselves? A quiet weekend in some country retreat without the presence of any members of their entourages might be a most productive exercise. If the next meeting is in Nairobi all the leaders should go to Treetops for the weekend and just sit about and talk.

The Commonwealth is in the process of creating opportunities for world co-operation at the top that have never existed before in history. This 1969 conference has come as the Commonwealth enters the twenty-first year of its modern existence (India became a republic and remained a member in April 1949). In those flu-ridden January days the Commonwealth demonstrated that it had in fact grown up. The future is full of exciting possibilities.

* Heads of Government spent the weekend at the British Prime Minister's country home Chequers while their Foreign Ministers went to the British Foreign Secretary's country home Dorneywood.

CHAPTER FOUR

1969: Fleet Street in Search of the Empire

The Commonwealth received a very bad press in Britain during the Sixties. The public did not understand the rapid change from Empire to Commonwealth that had taken place and Fleet Street tended to confuse and inflame rather than enlighten. It was a reflection in part at least of Britain's bewilderment at finding that its place in the world was now as a medium, rather than as a great, power. Having given its colonies independence there was a resentment that the leaders of the new countries now had views of their own and were putting them forcefully.

Today the Commonwealth gets a better press in many parts of the world; British newspapers remain unenthusiastic, though less hostile. Understanding of the Commonwealth among the mass of British people remains small.

After the 1969 Commonwealth conference in London—the last to be held in Britain for eight years—this article appeared anonymously* in the Round Table. It is included in this volume because it gives an impression of public opinion and attitudes at that time . . .

---

*It was in fact written jointly by the Editor, the late Leonard Beaton, and myself.

THE COMMONWEALTH PRIME Ministers' Meeting in London in January was a remarkable experience for many people. One of the greatest assemblages of heads of government since the San Francisco Conference of 1945 attracted the attention of the world and noticeably impressed its participants. It provoked some argument and many conflicting emotions. Nowhere was the response more confused and uncomprehending than in the British press, most of which predicted a repetition of the deep conflicts of 1966 and some of which became vigorously hostile to the whole Commonwealth association. Battles, rows, walk-outs, denunciations were predicted and from time to time reported throughout the Conference. In retrospect it makes an interesting commentary on the evolution of the British view of the world.

The conference began on 7 January. In the days leading up to it speculation centred on how the Rhodesian situation would be handled.

COMMONWEALTH STORM CERTAIN ON RHODESIA

said *The Times* over three columns. The *Daily Telegraph* said two days later that the Rhodesian situation 'threatens to split the conference asunder'. The *Daily Mirror* said that

African leaders are planning an all-out attempt to tie Premier Harold Wilson's hands on the future of Rhodesia.

The Observer had a dire prediction to offer:

The Rhodesian issue, despite preliminary efforts to whittle it down to size, will dominate the meeting. It could still be the rock on which the conference (and the Commonwealth itself) will founder.

Just before the conference began, the *Daily Mirror* relented and produced a surprisingly optimistic forecast:

The PM's Conference (despite the surface gloom) promises a new pattern of co-operation and understanding among the leaders. . . . It looks like the launching of Commonwealth Mark II.

The traditionally imperialist *Sunday Express* shed a tear for old memories:

Should we roll out the red carpet and cheer when the Commonwealth leaders arrive in London this week? Sadly, no. For the truth is that several of those who are coming have not the slightest loyalty either to Britain or the Commonwealth.

The nominees for this were Dr Kaunda and Mrs Gandhi. The

Daily Telegraph read the conference a stern lecture about not trying to push Britain around and urged Mr Wilson to walk out if he was subject to 'unreasonable pressure' on Rhodesia.

At a time when Britain needs clear-sightedness and self-confidence, the Commonwealth contributes to the pervasion of public life with a miasma of uncertainty and humbug. Traditional British moral assets, aspirations and standards are devalued by the pretence that they are shared by Commonwealth countries whose whole ethos may be different.

From the still farther right, the *Daily Sketch* had made up its mind that Britain was going to be attacked by 'this Commonwealth we've sired'.

The Commonwealth of today has become a voiceless visionless collection of self-seeking states. Its conferences have degenerated into ever more spiteful charades. . . . The Commonwealth, as it now exists, should be wound up.

Of the nine British national newspapers (excluding the Communist *Morning Star*), the *Financial Times* was outstanding for consistency, accuracy and imperviousness to the rumours of disaster. The socialist *Sun* was also willing to believe that things were indeed going as well as the Commonwealth Secretariat had predicted.

Nobody has to turn up in London for a week of discussion. Yet all 28 members will be represented—six of them newly independent and newly joined since the last meeting in 1966. It is an astonishing phenomenon, which has endured long enough for everybody to stop being surprised. If the Commonwealth had no value, the repeated prophecies of collapse would have come true.

The Times was modestly welcoming:

In the past 20 years the Commonwealth has cushioned Britain from many political shocks, and that may well include a Rhodesian debacle. It is true that the trend of British policy is away from the old Commonwealth ties. The loosening is general. But even now Commonwealth membership more often promotes or coincides with British interests than cuts across them.

The hunger for an atmosphere of row and showdown was satisfied on the opening day in most newspapers by a promise of a crisis over the fate of the East African Asians who were United Kingdom citizens. WILSON FACES ATTACKS OVER ASIANS said the *Daily Mirror*. SHOWDOWN OVER 30,000 ASIANS said the

45

Daily Mail. The *Daily Telegraph* summed up its view of the matter in the heading on its leader: COMMONWEALTH RACISTS. The Conference did produce a vigorous debate on this question and even, thanks to a clumsy British leak, some bad feeling. But the showdown never came.

The dynamite had to be somewhere. If not the East Africa Asians, then Rhodesia. *The Guardian* introduced the third day with

> The success or failure of the Commonwealth conference hangs in the balance today when Rhodesia is debated.

The *Daily Mail* revealed that

> A new hard-line plan on Rhodesia was prepared by African leaders last night before President Kaunda met Mr Wilson. The plan demands a tougher stand against Prime Minister Ian Smith than was shown on the Fearless. . . . Accusations that an 'Afro-Asian caucus' is running the conference are sure to be renewed at tomorrow's debate.

The *Daily Sketch* decided to devote its front page to the views of a non-member of the conference, Mr Enoch Powell, a former Conservative minister.

> Mr. Enoch Powell said last night that the Commonwealth had outlived its usefulness. 'It is a kind of humbug and self-deception which does more harm than good,' he declared.

The two-day Rhodesian debate did not live up to the Press's expectations. The words storm, row, attack, assault and so on got extensive use in the reports. But *The Guardian* produced an exotic account of the affair which excelled all others.

> Mr. Wilson and Dr. Kaunda emerged yesterday as the Achilles and the Hercules of this 1969 summit. They slogged it out toe to toe in two major policy speeches, each carefully drafted and lasting more than one hour. At the end, each withdrew warily, sheathing his sword until Wednesday, while the other 26 prime ministers and presidents around the long mahogany table rose anxiously from their chairs, wondering whether the club is about to tear itself apart.

It had in fact been a calm and much-praised debate in which all schools of opinion had emphasized their readiness to respect the views of others.

By the weekend, there was a growing shortage of political disputes to keep the press fuelled. The *Sunday Telegraph*, however, had a new revelation:

Meanwhile the jollifications, the receptions and dinners, which some Prime Ministers see as good enough reasons in themselves for keeping Commonwealth conferences going, broke all previous records. It is estimated that the rate of consumption of champagne at a Lancaster House party given by Mr. Wilson from 10 p.m. last Thursday until 1.30 a.m. on Friday was greater than at any two or possibly three other conference receptions.

A number of newspapers reported what the *Daily Mirror* described as 'a major struggle' over the writing of the communiqué, a lengthy and exhaustive document which certainly involved substantial discussion among the twenty-eight governments who were committing themselves to it. At the end of it all, *The Times* had almost nothing to say except that 'the Prime Ministers came to confer, and they did'. The *Sun* reported, accurately, that they had been 'borne along on a tide of unprecedented mutual goodwill' in agreeing the communiqueé.

The *Daily Telegraph* could stand it no longer:

> Another Commonwealth conference has come and gone, more hot and often noisome air has been blown, and a querulous communiqué has been issued. . . . Few maintain any longer that this association meeting in conference, is anything but a harmful nuisance to Britain's own interests. . . . Hard as it may seem, the United Kingdom would do best to withdraw from the association. . . . The wrench in practice would not be painful. It would free Britain from many embarrassments, illusions and distortions of her political and economic rule.

The *Spectator* took a similar line:

> On the eve of the conference . . . we argued that the time had come for Britain to leave the Commonwealth. Now that the past two weeks have shown that a number of Commonwealth countries are determined to persist in their maltreatment of British citizens, while the rest stand idly by, no other honourable course remains.

The *Daily Mail*, which only a short while before the conference had dropped the slogan 'For Queen and Commonwealth' from its masthead, was particularly scornful under the leader heading THE CIRCUS LEAVES TOWN.

> Thank heavens the Commonwealth Prime Ministers conference does not happen all that often. A week is quite long enough for Britain to stand in the pillory. We need a respite to wipe the rotten egg off our faces. . . The net effect of the whole shenanigan is that the British people think even less of the Commonwealth than they did before. As familiarity breeds so much contempt, would it not be better to hold the

conference in other Commonwealth capitals in future? If this circus is to continue, let it at least be a travelling circus.

When Mr Wilson reported on the conference to the House of Commons a few days later, the *Daily Telegraph* took up its hostility again. In a Page One report headed MPs HOOKED ON PREMIERS' 'HASH', it said:

> Mr. Heath and his followers . . . were eager to praise the Commonwealth. Even the leaders of the newest nations, he said, had left London convinced of the institution's value. Come to that, who would not value links with a country which offered you cheap loans, advantageous trade terms, periodic binges in London and promised to put up with any abuse you heaped on it?

With that, Fleet Street moved on to more familiar themes.

CHAPTER FIVE
Singapore 1971: To the Brink

A calm political atmosphere prevailed within the Commonwealth for the following 18 months, and the next Heads of
Government meeting planned for Singapore in January 1971
promised to be a productive one. But when a Conservative
Government unexpectedly came to power in Britain in June
1970 a change of policy on South Africa brought the
Commonwealth to the brink of collapse. These reports
describe the events leading up to the Singapore conference
of January 1971 and what happened at that cliff-hanger of a
meeting . . .

TO THOSE WHO, for one reason or another, spend so much of their time nursing a death-wish about the Commonwealth, the message of Singapore is this: The Commonwealth is not going to lie down and die. The Singapore Foreign Minister, Mr S. Rajaratnam, summed it up on the last day when he said that the only possible headline that should emerge at the end of the conference was, 'The Commonwealth declines to fall'. He said: 'A failing in the past had been that we have tended to conceive of it as a perfect Commonwealth. In the Seventies we should replace that concept with that of the imperfect Commonwealth. All we can hope to achieve, as in every other human endeavour, is a less imperfect Commonwealth but one which will always remain an imperfect Commonwealth.'

The sensible verdict on Singapore must surely be this: better than most Commonwealth *afficionados* dared to expect in the worrying days of the arms sales statements of July and August, much less satisfactory than the 1969 conference or than seemed likely when the talks were planned at the beginning of 1970. The Commonwealth experience of 1971 has not been something over which anyone can exult. It has shown us that the improved political climate between Commonwealth countries that sprang from the 1969 talks was not something that had necessarily come to stay.

In clarifying their minds about the current nature of the Commonwealth relationship, the delegates could take into account the fact that the association is now settling down in terms of numbers. It has grown by another three nations since 1969, but by 1975 it is unlikely that it will exceed thirty-five or thirty-six in number*—only four more than at present. Two-thirds of the Heads of Government at Singapore had met at a Commonwealth conference before—and that in itself demonstrated the considerable stabilization of the last few years.

To put the Singapore conference in proper perspective we need to recall the circumstances of the 1969 meeting. That conference had seemed a real turning point, and the warm atmosphere prevailed at subsequent Commonwealth gatherings—at the Finance Ministers' annual conference at Port of Spain in the following September, for instance.

When, as instructed by the 1969 summit, Arnold Smith began to make his soundings about the timing and venue of the next con-

---

* It reached thirty-six in 1976.

ference the way seemed clear for a successful follow-through: a conference that would devote most of its time to constructive debate about the future and purpose of the Commonwealth and implement many non-political, non-controversial schemes of Commonwealth development that the Secretariat and other bodies had worked on for several years.

Politically, there were fewer divisive issues in sight than at any time for years. Rhodesia was still with us and stood ready to haunt the conference as a Commonwealth failure, but that situation had barely changed since January 1969, and what was said then applied equally a year later. The Nigerian civil war, which had gnawed consciences outside the 1969 conference, had ended, and immigration, which also generated some disagreeable moments on the fringes of the 1969 talks, did not now seem to be a major hazard—if only because no one really wanted his own skeleton rattled.

There was a general desire to hold the talks outside London. The 1969 conference would have taken place in Ottawa but for the retirement of Lester Pearson. The 1971 venue, Singapore, and the host, Lee Kuan Yew, could not have been bettered. There was a need to get the conference into Asia. An Asian presence would bring the Commonwealth closer home to two of the least enthusiastic members, India and Australia, and it would help to answer the Asian critics who complained that the Commonwealth seemed obsessed with African affairs.

Until Harold Wilson called his snap election in June 1970, then, the path to Singapore seemed strewn with orchids. The surprise accession to office of a Conservative Government totally changed the prospect. Repeated Tory oral pledges before the election to resume arms sales to South Africa (not, incidentally, set down in the Party's manifesto) had seemed to pose a Commonwealth problem for the future, but few had foreseen that the Conservatives would wish to carry out these controversial pledges so speedily.

Within three weeks of the Conservative victory, on 6 July, the Foreign and Commonwealth Secretary, Sir Alec Douglas-Home, announced the Government's 'intention' to sell arms, and at that moment there was thus inserted into the Singapore conference an issue as divisive as Ian Smith's UDI had been five years earlier. Now came something deeply disappointing so far as the development of the Commonwealth was concerned: the revival of all the old African threats to leave the Commonwealth. The days of African walkouts and boycotts had been receding.

51

The reason President Nyerere went back to a 'We'll-quit-the-Commonwealth' line (though the threat was never actually publicly made by him; it appeared in the government-owned *Standard* of Dar es Salaam) was that he felt the whole basis of the Commonwealth was now in danger of being undermined; the broken-relations move of 1965 had solved nothing. The months leading up to Singapore were cliff-hangers. At some moments it seemed that the conference might have to be postponed. Even Arnold Smith, not known for his pessimism, was sometimes near to despair about prospects for the five years of his newly-renewed second term as Secretary-General that lay ahead.

The British Government, first declaring before the three-month Parliamentary recess in July that no action on arms would be taken before an announcement was made to the House of Commons, and then talking to Commonwealth leaders all through the autumn months, found themselves faced with unpleasant alternatives. To announce a decision to sell arms before the Singapore conference would put the Commonwealth's very existence into jeopardy and not exactly commend itself to the conference host, Lee Kuan Yew. Britain's new Prime Minister, Mr Edward Heath, had arranged to make a goodwill visit to India to try to repair damage done to Indo-British relations during the Wilson government. A sell-arms decision before the visit would risk angering Mrs Gandhi and worsen, not improve, relations between the two countries.

So the point was reached, in November, when it became clear that any decision must come after the conference (no statement, in any case, could be made to the conference itself because of the commitment to the Commons). Additionally, the unrelenting pressure against arms sales within Britain—and within Whitehall—had not been without its effect.

In the end, there gathered in Singapore on 17 January representatives of all thirty-one governments, of which twenty-five were Heads of Government, a ratio only slightly below that of 1969. The absentees—Stevens of Sierra Leone, Williams of Trinidad, Gowon of Nigeria, Yahya of Pakistan, Gandhi of India, and Kenyatta of Kenya—were none of them absent in protest. All, with the exception of Kenyatta had domestic preoccupations. The turnout was good in numbers but disappointing in content. Seven out of ten people in the Commonwealth are Asians and nearly all of these are Indian or Pakistanis. The fact that the leader of neither country was present at the Commonwealth's first conference in

Asia was a big minus. Nigeria, too, is the biggest black African country and is about equal third with Britain in the table of Commonwealth countries. Gowon's presence would have been useful though Mr Arikpo, the Commissioner for External Affairs, was a good substitute and made sure Nigeria's voice was clearly heard.

The African leaders arrived in Singapore amid a spate of reports that they would walk out of the conference. From the outset they gave assurances that they would not do so, and all were true to their word. They had come for serious discussion, and they had brought with them, as had everyone else, a desire to preserve the Commonwealth. It was this unanimous view that the Commonwealth was worthwhile and must be kept in being that was the factor that saved Singapore from disaster.

If these top men felt, as so many people in Britain seem to feel, that the Commonwealth is really not any use and the quicker it is wound up the better, then the will to strive for some formula that will meet everyone's requirements, for some compromise that will not upset the association beyond repair, would not be there. The agreement, with little fuss, to take South African arms on the third day as a separate agenda item, thus giving three days of quiet discussion on other international matters beforehand and so at least getting everyone used to the other's faces, was a symptom of this general goodwill.

The acceptance of a Declaration of Principles* setting down a number of beliefs on matters of race, poverty and the freedom of the individual was a Commonwealth milestone. It is an imperfect document from an imperfect association and there is not a country of the Commonwealth—or probably of the world—which can honestly say that it is carrying out all the pledges that are set down there. But then what husband or wife can honestly say that he flawlessly obeys all his marriage vows? That does not prevent our having marriage services giving solemn undertakings and trying our human best to keep them.

What emerged, sadly, from Singapore again was the apparent failure of the British to understand the modern Commonwealth. The Prime Minister and many of his team seemed to behave as though they were surrounded by thirty enemies instead of thirty good friends. What they just could not seem to understand was that

* See Appendix.

criticisms of British policy on South African arms were being expressed in a mood of 'more in sorrow than in anger'; they were sincerely made because almost every Commonwealth country believed that it was not in Britain's interests to do what she said she wanted to do. When a friend tries to tell you that you are wrong he is trying to be helpful not hostile. He is not trying to push you around. The fact that thirty countries care desperately what Britain does is a tribute to her, not an attack on her.

At the same time, Trudeau of Canada struck the right note when he said that both the British and the Africans were looking at the problem in the short term when really they should all be trying to work out what was likely to happen in Southern Africa in the years, not only the months ahead. But there was absolutely no need for the British to have felt that they were being pushed around. The whole purpose of diplomacy is to influence one another. Otherwise everyone might as well always stay at home.

The symptoms only too present among the British delegation in Singapore were not new; they were there during the Wilson government. This is not a question of party attitudes. It is a question of a national attitude of mind which reflected itself in Singapore by a display of semi-self-isolation. Britain seemed not to come to the conference table feeling 'Here are some problems to thrash out—let's see what we can all do together to work towards solutions', but rather that she had nothing to learn from the countries arraigned round the table; it was the others that needed to be educated. The tense and unrelaxed manner of the entire British delegation was most worrying to observe.

It was worrying, for instance, when Mr Heath went off on the Sunday sailing with some local Europeans, apparently taking no opportunity to spend some of the day with one or more of the thirty Commonwealth leaders in town. It is not often that so many top political figures are gathered together in one place, and the fact that the British Prime Minister chose not to unbend and spend part of the day with some of his Commonwealth colleagues was disturbing. The week-end that falls during these conferences should be used for informal get-togethers. In past years when the conference was held in London, it was the habit to hold talks at Chequers. Ideally the heads of delegations should go off together into some country retreat and chat and eat and drink and bathe and play golf. The Commonwealth needs to move back into much more informality both in its conference proceedings and in its off-duty moments. At

Singapore there was far too much smell of the United Nations around.

Basically, the problem was that the same arrangements cannot be made for thirty-one Presidents and Prime Ministers as obtained for fewer than a dozen a decade or so ago. The association has proliferated, and with that development have come a lot more officials and a lot more bumph. Not surprisingly, a Commonwealth Parkinson has been at work.

The essence of Commonwealth summit conferences has always been their informality and their secrecy. They are supposed to allow discussion to take place among the top men without fear that what each says will appear in print the next day; theoretically, the delegates are relieved of the need to posture and argue with half an eye on their own domestic political scene. Afterwards, it is for them to assure their parliaments that they have done right by their country and to put on their reports what political gloss they think appropriate.

For some years there have been disturbing trends in the format of Commonwealth conferences. It is easy (but wrong) to put much of the blame on the influx of African countries; a short experience of international conferences might well be held to have led their officials to assume that meetings of the Commonwealth were not so different from those of the United Nations and the Organization of African Unity. It would be possible, too (but also wrong), to level criticism at the Commonwealth Secretariat. The Secretariat's central dilemma is how to run a Commonwealth that has no wish to be institutionalized: on a loose rein that is not so loose as to be ineffective. A charge of 'UN-nery' at Singapore could be levelled against Lee Kuan Yew. As conference host the final organizational word lay with him, and his decision to build an oval table something like sixty feet long and thirty-five feet across with a hollow centre large enough to take a lorry load of tropical pot plants helped considerably to strip the meeting of intimacy.

At Marlborough House the table is long and narrow. It was, in 1969, admittedly too small for thirty places,* but it did mean that Premier Trudeau of Canada and President Nyerere of Tanzania could wink at each other across the table—and even pass a clandestine word or two to each other. At Singapore winking was right out; delegates sitting opposite each other were thirty feet and a

---

* Twenty-eight countries plus the host country's Foreign Minister and the Commonwealth Secretary-General.

55

dozen pot plants apart. (In fairness, it must be added that the long table also has its disadvantages—delegates cannot see the faces of those seated far down on their own side.)

Then there is the great number of officials. In 1969 each Head of Government was entitled to three assistants. In Singapore the number went up to four: a mixture of Ministers and civil servants, though if one Minister or another decided to take the afternoon off to shop for batik shirts all might be civil servants. Thus we had a room containing up to 200 people, many of whom would be wandering in and out during the debates. Delegates' badges, which did not (like the press passes) carry photographs, were to a certain extent interchangeable and so the number of people who could take up vacant chairs in this 'secret' conference might be estimated conservatively at 300. And lest it be thought that the Afro-Asians have been responsible for the increasing number of officials at the table, it is worth putting on record that Britain wanted six officials to sit with Mr Heath at Singapore. The British, therefore, take responsibility, too, for the drift to 'UN-nery'.

A further problem is that of set speeches. At Singapore there were scores. The habit has now developed of preparing long speeches that were (if the speaker so desires, and now he nearly always does) distributed to journalists after delivery. The discussions are thus robbed of much of their value; they have little spontaneity. In Singapore the international review and the economic debate suffered from these prepared tests. As Prime Minister Pierre Trudeau of Canada said at a press conference:

> On the economic item . . . I made some very few points from disjointed notes and I said that the reason why I hadn't spoken on the first item was because everybody came with long set speeches of the type that one delivers at the United Nations and I suggested that if we were going to do much of that we may as well create the convention of writing our speeches and autographing them and having them handed around and taking them as read. . . . We didn't have to travel thousands of miles to sit for hours listening to (these) speeches. . . .

The worst of all worlds came in the almost all-night full session on South African arms on 20-21 January. Delegates had arrived in Singapore with set speeches for this debate which they put away in drawers when it was decided to hold a secret session of the Heads of Government and Secretary-General Arnold Smith only.

In the secret meetings, which took place over twelve hours on 19 and 20 January, the conference did get back to its roots. Here were thirty-one men and one woman (Mrs Bandaranaike) locked in a much smaller room, seated round a square table, with a hollow centre, without microphones and free at last to speak their minds and to thrash out some acceptable formula.

Trudeau again:

> Between the meetings in the big room and the meetings in the small one, I found a tremendous difference. There was a great deal of question and answer and trying to get to the bottom of the other person's position, and it was very worthwhile.

The formula finally agreed at these long secret sessions was a face-saving one: Commonwealth countries would set up an Indian Ocean Study Group to examine the defence situation in the area. Britain's main argument all along had been that South African bases were vital if growing Soviet influence in the Indian Ocean was to be contained or at least balanced. Nine Commonwealth countries are littoral states and were also anxious that the Ocean should not become dominated by a single power.*

Regardless of all that had happened in the closed sessions, the delegates insisted on reading out their prepared speeches. President Banda of Malawi spoke for one hour after two o'clock in the morning.

It was this long session, more than anything else, which threw out the conference timetable and reduced the time available for the remaining agenda items. Mr Lee had considered, along with the Secretary-General, ruling that the prepared speeches would be taken as read, recorded in the conference official report, and issued to the press if delegates so wanted. He decided that so many Heads of Government wanted to deliver these speeches that it would be unwise to try to frustrate that desire.

Many African leaders felt very strongly the need to make their views clearly known. They felt the British were not being backward in making sure their case was well publicized, and their feelings were correct. British press briefings at Singapore were as adroit as any. But it is still difficult to understand how the actual delivery of these speeches made any difference to the resultant publicity, and

---

* The Group never met. There were disputes over membership and the British, having by now realized that it would be better for them not to supply arms to South Africa in any substantial amounts (the South Africans particularly wanted ships) played Pretoria along and in the end supplied only a few helicopters. See following Chapter.

the conference wearied itself from 8.30 p.m. till 3.55 a.m. listening to all the arguments that had already been made in the secret sessions (and at numerous Singapore press conferences).

All the same, it is important to focus correctly on Singapore. Of seven and a half days of talking only two were taken up with the South African arms item; as usual, press concentration on one topic has given a rather misleading picture.

Mr Heath did not enjoy Singapore and there was no reason why he should since he had chosen the previous July to insert into the conference a thoroughly divisive issue. He was almost totally alone among the thirty-one Presidents and Prime Ministers (even Australian support was not always wholehearted), and he and his officials marched about outside the conference room as men apart—almost, one delegate said, like Peter Sellers and his shop stewards in the film 'I'm All Right, Jack.' Even allowing for Heath's jaundiced attitude, it is plain that many of his views on the development of 'UN-nery' in the Commonwealth were almost unanimously shared.

Prime Minister Forbes Burnham of Guyana suggested that the Secretariat should make a study of changes of procedure and this went forward.

The most important single factor about Singapore was that not one President or Prime Minister wanted to see the Commonwealth disappear. The will to strengthen it and make it more useful, not less, was there, and many of the leaders present like Premiers Shearer of Jamaica, Trudeau of Canada, and Gorton of Australia, Mr Arikpo of Nigeria, and Presidents Nyerere and Kaunda worked hard and with real feeling for the Commonwealth. Indeed, the ironic fact is that the Commonwealth now seems to be better understood by the leaders of the newer countries than it is by those of Britain.

In the last two days there had seemed to be a realization that the trend to 'UN-nery' needed to be arrested. One official said: 'Suddenly everyone seemed to feel a little ashamed—this really wasn't the way the Commonwealth ought to be behaving.'

Proof of this new mood came in the decision to issue a shorter communiqué. Two versions had been prepared. One was 1969-length—several thousand words. The other was just over 1,000 words. The conference chose the short one. It was a hopeful pointer to the future.

CHAPTER SIX

1971–3: Convalescence between Singapore and Ottawa

Following the near-disaster of Singapore member governments and the Secretariat gave much thought to ways in which the Commonwealth should now develop and how Heads of Government meetings should be conducted in future. The next host country, Canada, in particular was painstakingly thorough in working out the right formula for success. Canada's Prime Minister, Pierre Trudeau, set his Special Assistant, Ivan Head, about the task of sounding out Commonwealth Governments on the proposed conference. Head went to every one of the (then) thirty-two Commonwealth countries. It took him three months and in only two of the thirty-two did he not see the Head of Government. In both cases there was a 'justifiable reason'.

Midway between the two conferences I was asked to deliver a lecture on the situation of the Commonwealth as it had emerged after the Singapore experience. These are extracts from the lecture given at the Royal Commonwealth Society's headquarters in London and from an article written just before the Ottawa conference assessing the constructive results of Singapore.

HERE WE ARE now well away from the decolonization of the Fifties and Sixties, poised probably almost exactly midway between those heads of government conferences, during which the Commonwealth captures the headlines for a few days and is then half-forgotten, and also almost certainly only a few months off British entry into the European Common Market. We have just seen a member country (Pakistan) of almost twenty-five years' standing leave the Commonwealth* and we have seen a country (Bangladesh) apply to join.† It has been demonstrated for all to see that the Commonwealth is very much the voluntary association the cliché has always claimed it to be, and that it is indeed a club of countries in which no single member has the dominant voice.

For a long time now the Commonwealth has been a favourite whipping boy for all and sundry, usually suffering on the one hand from charges that it is the tool of Whitehall, and on the other being treated with varying degrees of indifference by succeeding British governments. It has, for instance, been a popular theory in some quarters in Britain in recent years that membership of the Commonwealth actually hinders Britain's freedom of action, that it was being prevented from pursuing policies that it thought were in its own interest because it was always having to take into consideration the views and desires of thirty other countries of the world, most of which belonged to the non-aligned groupings and therefore usually did not hold the same views as Britain.

Now surely we need to accept that membership of international bodies, whatever they are, does curtail certain freedom of action; it does, if you like, impinge on sovereignty. These bodies exist so that their members shall influence each other on common objectives, so that they *shall* try to achieve common policies which will require some give-and-take on all sides. Membership of the European Economic Community will involve us in a certain loss of sovereignty, though not more than we have already lost in membership of the host of international organizations to which Britain already belongs. They are simply different areas of sovereignty.

Membership of the Commonwealth does, or should, impose a certain need to change one's policies now and again so that they are more acceptable to the rest of the partners, and although we may be thinking at the moment of this point in a British context it also means that Tanzania or India or Nigeria or Jamaica must also be

* Pakistan left the Commonwealth on 30 January 1972.

† Bangladesh became a full member on 18 April 1972.

expected to consider what they are doing is helpful or unhelpful to the common good of all.

If we can accept that we are just beginning to move into this era of some shared sovereignty, that we are somehow groping towards a greater internationalism, then nations have to accept that they cannot always have their own way. They cannot act along a narrow lane of self-interest, but must consider with sympathy the other's point of view and try to meet it.

The Commonwealth is perhaps able to illustrate this to the world and to serve as a prototype of something greater in the decades to come, for it is not a group that has within it any super-power. Some would say that renders it rather ineffectual; I would suggest it might be otherwise. The fact that it contains something like a quarter of the world's states and something like a quarter of the world's peoples and yet lacks all three super-powers, could be a strength. It offers at least a wonderful flexibility.

If we examine recent events we can see how British policy has been changed to a certain extent because of the existence of the Commonwealth. Governments are good at giving an impression that they are doing one thing while they are in fact doing the opposite. The recent rumpus over South Africa is interesting in this context. The fusing of the proposition to resume arms sales was something we knew everything about. But the defusing of the proposition is something which has had much less attention.

The fact is that most people, delegates as well as observers, left the Singapore Commonwealth conference in January 1971 convinced that the arguments against arms sales made there had fallen on deaf ears, that nothing would deter Britain from going ahead. The African leaders and all those who supported them felt that they had made no inroads with their case. But it was not so. They had at least eroded the British plans. It was the Commonwealth that won on points in Singapore, though you would not have believed it at the time. Remember, after hours of argument a formula was found that got the British and everyone else off the hook—the magic Indian Ocean Study Group. The British said they retained the right to their own freedom of action and promptly announced the sale of Wasp helicopters. Nearly two years after the whole rumpus began and fifteen months after the Commonwealth conference no ships are being built or are ordered and sales remain at those seven helicopters, which I gather will now be completed in a year's time and will in due course be granted an export licence and supplied. This is

61

the sum total of the order with Britain and nothing else as far as we know is on the stocks direct.

There *were* second thoughts and in the end it was at least partially realized that it was not in the common interest and therefore not in the British interest to go ahead. Of course, the South Africans helped to change British minds by getting nervous about the amount of African uproar Britain's involvement was creating, but the Commonwealth acted as a brake, and while there will be some of the far right who will say that this was a good argument for not having a Commonwealth, most thinking people will see it as a powerful case *for* the Commonwealth.

If other countries can influence British policy it is also the case that Britain can influence Commonwealth countries—and it seems an odd thing to have to say, but in many ways these days Britain does not take enough advantage of the Commonwealth connection to propagate its views and to exert an influence.

A question that needs serious attention is whether the Commonwealth is really an association for small countries-only. It is not without significance that by and large the smaller countries of the Commonwealth have in the last few years shown more enthusiasm for it than the bigger ones. The real problem members of the Commonwealth recently have been Britain, India and Australia. Canada has always played a leading and constructive role and so has New Zealand, but we tend to forget that New Zealand is one of the smallest members, having a population only about one-third of that of Ghana, for instance.

I always find it galling when people in Britain refer scornfully to the newer Commonwealth countries with the remark: 'Of course, they are only in the Commonwealth for what they can get out of it.' I always say: 'Of course, and quite right too. What sort of fool belongs to a club if he doesn't get anything out of it?' The Commonwealth is no good to any member unless it is getting something out of it. And this is where the test comes. For a small country like Botswana there is plenty to get out of the Commonwealth. Organizations like the Commonwealth Fund for Technical Co-operation (CFTC) can give great help to such a country. The service of international position papers and advice in economic fields that the Commonwealth Secretariat provides is of immense value. At Commonwealth summit conferences the President or Prime Minister is able to meet many world leaders, at a stroke, as they say these days. It enables him to understand trends and policies in parts of the world far from his own. It helps him to be in the international swim in a way that might not be so easy if his country was not in the Commonwealth.

But these are things which are not of particular value to nations like Britain and Canada—indeed these countries usually have to make some small financial contribution—and in a country like India, though there are specialist fields in which organizations like the CFTC might make a substantial contribution, it is perhaps too much like a pebble thrown into the great spaces of the subcontinent to weigh in Delhi as a reason for membership of the Commonwealth.

It is India's indifference to the Commonwealth that has been almost the most worrying factor of all in recent years, for India is in a special position in the Commonwealth; in the first place it is, after all, because of India's decision to remain a member as a republic in 1949 that there is a Commonwealth at all. And then also because India, by historical accident, is the country that has more of its culture and its peoples planted around the Commonwealth than any other country except Britain—Indian communities in Africa, in Fiji, in Mauritius, in the Caribbean and so forth. These communities are not in non-Commonwealth countries—they are in Commonwealth countries. And so India does have wide and deep connections with the Commonwealth.

India could use the Commonwealth machine and Commonwealth channels in a much more positive way in furthering its ideas on such pressing problems as population control or pollution or the scramble by the big powers for international control of the mineral riches on the seabed. The Commonwealth constitutes a considerable slice of votes at the United Nations and a common approach on such subjects in New York—and Indian initiatives in achieving such a common approach—could not help but be of benefit to India herself as well as to everyone else.

In recent years Indian initiatives in the Commonwealth have been rare and muted, and Indian attitudes have been coloured by whatever the current state of Anglo-British relations. This has betrayed a fundamental failure to grasp the fact that the Commonwealth is not a bilateral relationship between India and Britain but a multilateral one between India and thirty other countries, of which Britain is one. For several years until recently, relations between our two countries were strained and the consequent attitude to the Commonwealth was one of indifference and even hostility. But on a visit to India recently I found Indians saying that never since independence had the Commonwealth been held in more favour. While this is a most pleasing development, it is also, as far as one can gather, again partly for the wrong reasons. It is because relations with Britain have become happier and because Britain and the old Commonwealth countries came to India's support unhesitatingly in the crisis last year and supported the establishment of Bangladesh.

Ever since 1947 the Indo-Pakistan rivalry has cast a deep shadow across the Commonwealth. It has been an important factor in shaping Indian attitudes to the Commonwealth. After all, what could the ordinary man make of an association of states dedicated to co-operation between colours and creeds and nations which contained two major members that were seldom on speaking terms and had once or twice been on fighting terms with each other?

Thus the departure of Pakistan from the Commonwealth, regrettable as it is in theory, could turn out in practice to be a strengthener.* The Indo-Pakistan situation has been a sore on the Commonwealth face and that is now removed. Conversely, the fact that Bangladesh considers it important to join the Commonwealth is itself a demonstration to all the doubters that the association must be something worthwhile.

It is being said vaguely that by leaving the Commonwealth Pakistan will lose little except some educational help. This is a false picture—there are to begin with about 270 Commonwealth organizations from which Pakistan will have to withdraw and to be seen to withdraw. To quote just a few examples at random. Pakistan will be cut off from the preferential system under the Commonwealth postal agreement and removed from the Commonwealth Telecommunications Board arrangements. Students, postgraduates and university staff from Pakistan will no longer benefit from the Commonwealth-wide and highly successful Scholarship and Fellowship plan. It will be removed from the Association of Commonwealth Universities. It will no longer benefit from all those fields in which the Commonwealth Secretariat brings Commonwealth countries together to discuss problems of finance, trade, aid, commodities, sterling, banking, medicine, youth, tourism, drugs—to name only a few. Professional people in

* An argument that has not been sustained. In the way political patterns change in that area of the world Bangladesh is at the time of writing in dispute with India again and on better terms with Pakistan.

64

Pakistan will no longer benefit from the work of the Commonwealth Foundation.

Simple convincing facts about the Commonwealth are always difficult to put to the sceptic sufficiently briefly to have any effect. But by now it must have occurred to some of these doubters that the durability of the Commonwealth has proved itself. When we look on all the change of the last fifteen years, all the crises through which it has pulled, it must have dawned on most people who really think about it for a while that the base of it is firmer than most people imagine.

I know there are still many who consider that the Commonwealth has been a disappointment as an institution and that it has not lived up to its promise. Some who have turned against it in recent years are people who expected spectacular results in a very short time. High expectations, and failure of those expectations, have led to disillusion. But if these people were only to consider the situation more calmly they would reflect that it is surely remarkable that after the last twenty years of total change, of changes of constitution, of changes of leadership to men and women of different philosophies and temperaments, of periods of deep world crisis like Suez or Cuba, of fierce internal conflicts, that the Commonwealth is still in existence, with very little change indeed in its original composition.

There are many more Commonwealth meetings in non-controversial fields going on today than there were ten years ago. There is much closer co-operation in these areas than used to be the case. There is co-operation on subjects which no-one thought about at one time.

At the Commonwealth Secretariat Headquarters in Marlborough House some considerable international figures have applied their minds to making the Commonwealth a practical association in modern terms and the results of all this work, set down in many reports and papers produced by the Secretariat, make impressive reading. It is not their fault that the message is not getting down to the peoples of the Commonwealth, though at last this problem is being tackled on a limited basis in the new Commonwealth information programme.

To those who expected the Commonwealth to be a nice tight bloc of countries acting together and solving half the world's problems over-night the Commonwealth is a disappointment, as must be all international organizations from the United Nations downwards. It is not the fault of the Commonwealth; it is the fault of mankind.

What the Commonwealth really needs to chalk up is one really major diplomatic achievement, and this so far it has not managed to achieve. It brought the parties together in the Nigerian civil war, but the war went on for more than a year longer. It was not able to grasp the Indo-Pakistan problem—and little wonder, having seen what has happened since. It has largely failed in grasping the vexed problems of migration and movement of population, though in time it might still be able to help to overcome some sensitivities in this field.

But meantime, there is much more that can be done. The Commonwealth has in the last few years carried out a most important study on the problems of youth employment and the drift of young people from the rural areas to the cities. At a series of conferences held in Nairobi, Port-of-Spain, and Kuala Lumpur, it has looked at the problem as it exists in Africa, in the Caribbean, in the South-East Asia and South Pacific areas. The exchange of ideas on a problem that is worrying governments in different shapes and forms all over the world could prove of just as much value to countries outside the Commonwealth as within it, and this is where the close liaison that is maintained by the Secretariat with the United Nations and other international organizations can show its worth.

That exercise on youth is now well on its way to completion and the time will come for the Commonwealth to look for another similar subject that can be studied in this way, area by area. It has seemed to some who are interested in Commonwealth developments that a most valuable study could be made into the whole question of the future of the English language. As a language of communication throughout the world, English grows all the time, and there seems little doubt that, without any conscious forces pressing English for sinister or neo-colonial reasons but just because of a natural impetus over the years, it will remain the major international language.

But as the language is taught from one generation to another in those countries where it is not the indigenous language, local pronunciation and usage tends to become more characteristic of the local people, and more widely different from usages elsewhere. The rate of divergence is widening fast so that people speaking English in one area of the world are likely to become almost unintelligible to each other. Indeed, in some cases, this has already happened. As

English is the language of the Commonwealth it would seem only appropriate that its preservation through the changed circumstances of Commonwealth countries should be the subject of a large-scale Commonwealth study.

Before the Ottawa conference in 1973 I looked back on what had actually been done in the Commonwealth in the thirty months that separated Singapore from Ottawa—the constructive but unspectacular work that flowed from that fraught conference of 1971 . . .

It is frequently assumed that when Commonwealth Heads of Government meet they merely find themselves arguing about such contentious subjects as Rhodesia, South African arms or immigration and end up with little to show for their ten days or so of talking. But the main advantages of a conference like this one, as with most international gatherings, are intangible: the corridor and coffee room chats, the opportunities for a President or Prime Minister to meet new opposite numbers (and, as important, if not more so in many cases, the opportunities for officials to meet each other informally); chances to talk about bilateral as well as multilateral matters; and the changed nuances in strands of policy that flow, perhaps months later, from these personal encounters.

At each conference—however much one subject may be highlighted because of its transient newsworthiness—a considerable amount of other business important to the functional development of the Commonwealth is carried through. Classic examples were the twin major decisions to set up the Commonwealth Secretariat and the Commonwealth Foundation. These decisions were made at the Conferences in 1964 and 1965 in London. Neither development received much attention at the time because Rhodesia was the topic that caught popular interest.

In 1971 at Singapore the subject of arms for South Africa dominated the conference and did in fact squeeze out important discussion on some other matters. Nonetheless, notable Commonwealth initiatives reached the point of decision and have been acted on. New activities in three fields sprang from Singapore—on the technical aid front, in youth work and in information.

A pilot programme of technical assistance on a Commonwealth basis had been in existence since 1967. Experience of this had shown that, without duplicating existing international aid arrangements, there was a need for a scheme that would be able to match individual technical talents to particular individual prospects and at the same time be sufficiently mobile and flexible to meet urgent requests at short notice. A Canadian, Mr George Kidd, was therefore installed as manager of a new Commonwealth Fund for Technical Co-operation (CFTC) with a team of experts from six countries and they have already done much valuable work. They were able, for example, to offer prompt help to Bangladesh in planning an export programme; they were able to help Zambia in organizing airlift and road transport operations following the closure of the Rhodesia border; and they have undertaken on request studies for individual Commonwealth countries on the likely impact on their trade and long-term economic situation of Britain's entry into the European Community. A range of projects, from mineral exploitation to port administration and from tourism surveys to manpower planning, have been carried out in twenty-five independent Commonwealth countries as well as in a number of associated states and dependent territories.

One source of the importance of the Fund lies in the way the concept cuts across the traditional pattern of developed and developing: it enables the developing to help the developing. Thus, under the education and training programme of the Fund, a radio producer from, say, Zambia, may take a course in Kenya or a foreign service officer from Fiji may attend a course in Trinidad.

The CFTC is off to a good start and Governments are showing confidence in it by increasing the flow of money. In the first year they provided only £400,000, in the second year £1 m—and 1973-4 is expected to show a further rise towards the eventual target of £2 million. At Singapore Australia stayed out of the Fund, but last year it came in with a sizeable contribution—an act that has helped to inject confidence into the scheme.*

The Commonwealth Youth Programme was another highly promising enterprise launched at Singapore. The first steps had been taken some years previously, and in 1969 the Heads of Government Conference held a first discussion on the subject. Study conferences had been held in each of the main regions of the Commonwealth to look at such trends as the drift of young people from country to town, bringing about a sense of disillusionment and

* Today the CFTC stands at £8 million and its work is expanding by the month. Contributions come from developing countries—the largest from Nigeria—as well as the developed. Canada matches contributions of developing countries on a two for one basis up to a given ceiling each year. Mr Kidd was succeeded as manager by Mr Anthony Tasker, from Britain.

rising delinquency. The object of the discussions was to discover ways to marshal the enthusiasms and initiatives of youth so that Commonwealth countries might benefit. At Singapore it was decided to conclude the studies and then to hold a Ministers' meeting to work out a Commonwealth programme. These talks were held in Lusaka, Zambia, in January 1973. Several imaginative ideas have emerged, including a Commonwealth Youth Award—an opportunity for groups of young people to show off projects they have devised to groups of young people in other Commonwealth countries. Zambia has offered to house the first regional Commonwealth Youth Centre and a Commonwealth Youth Information Service will help young people to learn about opportunities for study and work in other Commonwealth countries, and about programmes of exchange of youth workers and of leadership training.

The third major outcome of Singapore was the launching of the Commonwealth information programme. This was a step towards making the work and activity of the Commonwealth better known to the peoples of member countries. It was a move in the right direction, but the reluctance of some Governments to go along with the idea—particularly the Indian Government—has meant that the funds needed for a major publicity effort have been lacking. The programme, however, has made a good start; and Commonwealth activity is at last being recorded in a variety of publications—at one time information was so unco-ordinated that it was almost impossible to find out what Commonwealth conferences were happening in any given month. But the impact of all these efforts has yet to show through in any substantial way.

Another event that flowed from Singapore was the meeting of senior officials from Cabinet and Prime Ministers' Offices that took place in October 1972 in Ottawa to discuss 'Comparative Techniques of Government'—an idea put forward by Mr Trudeau, the Canadian Prime Minister, for discussion at Singapore. The item was crowded out at that meeting, but the Heads of Government decided that the notion was well worth exploring, and the Ottawa talks were a considerable success.

Mr Trudeau is concerned by what he called the challenge of developing democracy in a technological age; and he is convinced of the value of exchanging ideas on, and comparing experience in, methods of government. Subjects discussed at the Ottawa meeting included the relationship between the public service and the

Government, the implementation of Cabinet discussions, the improvement of communication between Government and people and the role of a cabinet office in co-ordinating submissions to the Cabinet. The turnout of top level officials at Ottawa was impressive and the consensus afterwards was highly favourable. Similar meetings are to be held on a regular basis, but meanwhile the Heads of Government will discuss the subject further at their meeting in August 1973.

At Singapore decisions were also taken to expand the scope of the Commonwealth Foundation and to launch a Commonwealth Book Development Scheme. The object of the Book Scheme is to help increase the supply of educational material to Commonwealth countries by overcoming problems of exchange control. A start has been made with a regional seminar in New Delhi and steps are being taken to set up an exchange voucher scheme for scientific and technical journals.

The amount of intra-Commonwealth activity in the thirty months between Singapore and Ottawa would seem to have been running at a record level. Something like ninety Commonwealth conferences, seminars, and other meetings have taken place, ranging from a regional meeting of planners and senior economists in Swaziland to a metrication conference in London, from a planning seminar on public examinations in Accra to the Third Medical Conference in Mauritius. The Commonwealth Heads of Government conferences, at the apex of all this cross-fertilization, provide the necessary stimulus; a replenishment of thought and ideas that helps the whole concept to feel its way forward.

CHAPTER SEVEN

Ottawa 1973: The Recipe for Success

The rethinking and careful preparation for the Heads of
Government meeting in Ottawa paid off. How the Commonwealth changed and engendered a new and much more constructive atmosphere among the leaders is traced in these
reports written before and after the conference.

FOR A NUMBER of reasons the meeting of Commonwealth Heads of Government that is to take place in Ottawa from 2–10 August could match in significance the meeting India, Pakistan and Ceylon attended as newly independent sovereign states in October 1948 under the chairmanship of Clement Attlee. Those first summit talks of a multi-racial Commonwealth ushered in a transitional period that has lasted a quarter of a century. A meeting of nine member countries convened by Britain has developed almost by accident (certainly not by any plan) into a meeting at which Britain is one of thirty-two participants.*

The Ottawa conference could also set the Commonwealth pattern for a long time to come. It will be held, incidentally, for the first time in the country which a century ago became the first territory in the British Empire to achieve self-government from Britain by mutual agreement. It will be the third conference held outside Britain and the first to be hosted by a member of, for want of a better phrase, the Old Commonwealth overseas. It will conduct its business in a more informal style than has been the case for many years and the Queen will be in attendance in Ottawa (though not, of course, participating) in her capacity as Head of the Commonwealth and Head of State of Canada—not as Head of State of the United Kingdom. Most significantly of all, perhaps, the conference is being held *after* British entry into the European Economic Community.

Indeed, when Commonwealth leaders sit down on 2 August for their meeting it will be only hours after the target date for the opening in Brussels of the complex and far-reaching economic negotiations involving up to sixty countries aimed at working out the future relationships with Western Europe of a large part of the developing world. Thus the conference meets at a good time, for it will follow a period in which all the public focus has been on Europe and when the relationship of the Commonwealth vis-à-vis Europe may begin to be seen in a less emotional perspective. The conference will publicly demonstrate that despite Britain's EEC membership the Commonwealth is still there.

When, in mid-1972, the time came to fix the exact date for the Heads of Government meeting in Ottawa, enthusiasm for the meeting among most countries had not waned—Trudeau was

---

* With the independence of the Bahamas on 10 July 1973, there were thirty three independent members of the Commonwealth. Nauru, however, does not attend Heads of Government meetings.

keener than ever despite a pending general election—but problems arose about dates. Mostly they were the usual ones—commitments to other international meetings like those of the UN General Assembly, the Organization of African Unity, non-aligned conferences and so forth—but the country that seemed to find all four suggested dates stretching from May to September inconvenient by turn was Britain. Eventually it agreed to early August, but the inescapable conclusion was that Prime Minister Edward Heath had no great enthusiasm for any Commonwealth meeting in 1973. (From time to time since Singapore the impression has been conveyed from official quarters that 'the Prime Minister might not attend the next meeting anyway—he might send the Foreign and Commonwealth Secretary' or 'perhaps he might come for only part of the time'.) It is true that Mr Heath has a busy year on his hands, with many extra commitments arising from British entry into the EEC, but his Singapore experience still rankles and the conclusion is inescapable that instead of seeing the opportunities that such a Commonwealth gathering presents to develop British foreign policy in the Third World he would rather the conference was not taking place.

The meeting, however, goes ahead, despite British faintheartedness, underlining Britain's changed position in the Commonwealth, and it is not without interest that there appeared to be no such doubts about the importance of the Commonwealth meeting at Buckingham Palace; all the indications were that the Queen was prepared to visit Ottawa at almost any time, despite the fact that she was already booked to go to Canada once in 1973, in June, for the Prince Edward Island centennial celebrations.

There is many a slip between the high promise of successful outcome that can exist at the inception of a Commonwealth conference and the actual meeting itself. The danger is always of some new issue blowing up in the interim period (which is what happened in 1971 as a result of the sudden insertion of the South African arms issue into the scene). Predictions about Ottawa have therefore to be cautious. Some unexploded mines are lying about and, as so often, they concern Africa. Whether the unpredictable President Amin of Uganda goes to Ottawa or not (it is sure to be much in his mind that he himself ousted President Obote while the latter was in Singapore for the last conference) his shadow is bound to be across the talks because of the British Asian headache he has given the United Kingdom government and because several Commonwealth

73

countries will also be wondering how Amin's actions can be reconciled with the Declaration of Commonwealth Principles they signed in Singapore, which says, inter alia:

> We recognise racial prejudice as a dangerous sickness threatening the healthy development of the human race and racial discrimination as an unmitigated evil of society. Each of us will vigorously combat this evil within our own nation. No country will afford to regimes which practice racial discrimination assistance which in its own judgment directly contributes to the pursuit or consolidation of this evil policy.

Immigration is an issue which the Commonwealth likes to shelve. Previous attempts at taking an overall look at the problems have always foundered (the 1969 conference in London agreed that a Commonwealth study should be undertaken, but the exercise made little progress because countries were reluctant to co-operate in supplying details). The real difficulty is that the subject smacks far too much of interference in internal affairs. For this reason alone there will be reluctance to raise the matter of Uganda's behaviour at Ottawa, even though Britain, India and several others are with good reason most disturbed about it.

Then there is as always—like Banquo's Ghost—Rhodesia. In 1969 the Commonwealth discussed Rhodesia in a tranquil and reasonable manner and at Singapore in 1971 the South African arms issue overshadowed the Rhodesian question. On both occasions the situation was stagnant. Since Singapore we have had the Smith-Home agreement and the Pearce Commission,* the result of which greatly comforted Commonwealth countries which felt that Britain, in a manner they had so often experienced in the past, had at least done the decent thing in the end: abided by the findings of a traditionally uncommitted and totally fair British judge. As long as there was no movement in the Rhodesian situation the Pearce Report was under the Commonwealth belt and an insurance against a sellout of the African people.

But at the beginning of 1973 there was again movement in the Central African situation and even indications that some fundamental change might be taking place. The African Commonwealth—and much of the rest—is again watching for any British weakening in dealing with Smith, and in the commitment to the

---

* In 1971 Sir Alec Douglas-Home, British Foreign and Commonwealth Secretary, agreed a Rhodesia Settlement with Ian Smith. But a commission set up under Lord Pearce to test African opinion decided that the Africans found the agreement unacceptable. The proposals were shelved.

principle of genuine African participation in any settlement. And, paradoxically, while a settlement with Smith may have become easier to sell in Britain it is going to be more difficult than ever to sell to the Commonwealth, for in the last year or so a major hardening of attitudes has taken place. The Africans now have much stronger support among Commonwealth countries. Their newest allies are Australia and New Zealand, whose just-elected Labour Governments have placed themselves firmly alongside Canada on this and similar issues. Jamaica, hitherto the most conservative of the Caribbean members, is now, under its new Prime Minister Mr Michael Manley, more militantly pro-African, the Ghanaian military government of Colonel Acheampong* has disowned Mr Busia's conciliatory line, and Nigeria, increasingly internationally minded as the civil war recedes into history, has no intention of letting down the Rhodesian Africans. Even the three Southern African Commonwealth countries, led by Botswana, have strengthened their positions on Rhodesia. The Nigerian view is especially important since Britain has for a long time been painstakingly repairing relations with Lagos and one of the prizes is a visit to Britain by General Gowon. Any Rhodesian settlement unfavourable to the Africans is bound to undo this work with the one African country that Britain really sees as vitally important to itself economically.

With luck these African difficulties on the way to Ottawa will not materialize. No one, including the Africans who, apart from President Amin, play diplomacy in a much more sophisticated, lower key manner these days than they did in the first years of independence, wants to see a confrontation with Britain at Ottawa—and all are aware of the value of making this a productive conference. It has every chance of being so.

The new format of the talks themselves should help greatly. At Singapore it was not only Mr Heath who felt that the informality of earlier years had been lost in a welter of officials and a large acreage of highly-polished table; Mr Trudeau had firm ideas about it and so did Mr Hugh Shearer, then Prime Minister of Jamaica. Mr Forbes Burnham, Prime Minister of Guyana, proposed on the last day of the Singapore talks that the Secretariat should study the problem, and the result has been a healthy reappraisal of all the procedures. This year will mark the beginning of a new style of

---

* On 13 January 1972 Col. Acheampong replaced Dr Busia's government in a coup d'état.

75

Commonwealth conference. It is likely, for example, that the full array of thirty-two Heads of Government and their officials (last time each had four assistants) will sit down only at the opening and closing sessions. Apart from these plenary meetings, the main business will in future be conducted in two kinds of session:

Executive: Normal working sessions on specific subjects, attended by the leaders and one or two officials at the most. (This will reduce the number in the room to something under 100.)

Restricted: Attended only by the thirty-two leaders and the Secretary-General of the Commonwealth, Arnold Smith. No record will be taken and no unauthorized statement will be made to press or TV

The idea is that in future there should be much more opportunity for impromptu intervention and spontaneous dialogue. Agendas, it has been recommended, should allow for a survey of major aspects of the international scene and intensive discussion of a few current questions such as development issues, pollution and population increase, the revolution of rising expectations, problems of alienation among the younger generation, problems of internal tension between communities distinguished by linguistic, religious and other characteristics. National issues of common concern should be discussed, but no single topic should dominate the conference.

Although there has been discussion about cutting out prepared texts and trying to limit the lengths of speeches, decisions on these points will be made when the Ottawa conference is convened. In fact, this further procedural streamlining will probably be the first item to be tackled.

The talks will take place in the Ottawa Conference Centre, until recently the city's main railway station. The hall in which the plenary session will be held was once the main concourse and is unsuitable for informal discussion. It has a soaring ceiling and delegates will need earphones. The much smaller executive room is being remodelled for the talks, while the room to be used for the restricted sessions, once the office of the Chairman of Canadian Pacific Railways, is smaller still and will contain just one round table to seat thirty-three people.

The introduction of the restricted session—Heads of Government only—as part of the programme instead of, as before, for emergencies only, is an important development that should prove rewarding. Very different discussion takes place when Presidents and Prime Ministers are on their own, with no note being taken and no officials present. It is coming back towards the kind of informal get-together that Prime Ministers had in the Forties and Fifties, though, of course, numbers must now always limit the intimacy in some degree. Paradoxically, while interest for the Common- wealth may at present be at a low ebb in Britain in general and in No 10 Downing Street and the Foreign and Commonwealth Office in particular, the association now gets a higher rating in Ottawa and Canberra than it did a few years ago. Mr Trudeau has admitted that when he became Prime Minister of Canada he regarded the Commonwealth with some scepticism; today he sees it as an important factor in Canadian foreign policy and he is hosting this year's conference because he believes in the Commonwealth and its possibilities for the future. He has described himself more than once as a 'deep convert' to the Commonwealth. Domestically, he sees it as something that distinguishes Canada's separate identity from America.

Despite the confused impressions to the contrary created by Australian moves to catch up with Canada and remove certain bilateral ties with Britain, Mr Gough Whitlam, the new Prime Minister of Australia, has a feeling for the modern Commonwealth that his predecessors—Holt, Gorton and McMahon—never had. All three had served as Ministers under Sir Robert Menzies and were influenced by his jaundiced view of the modern Common- wealth: that it had taken a wrong turning in becoming multi- racial, that the founding of the Secretariat was a mistake and that the choice of a Canadian as Secretary-General was unfortunate. Within days of Mr Whitlam's coming to power the whole picture had changed, with the new Prime Minister taking a special personal interest in Commonwealth affairs and conveying an invitation to Mr Arnold Smith to visit Australia as soon as possible. Mr Whitlam will find his attitudes strongly supported by New Zealand's new Prime Minister, Mr Norman Kirk. The Trudeau- Whitlam-Kirk team is going to look very different at Ottawa from the Trudeau-Gorton-Holyoake team at Singapore.

Yet the topic that is sure to dominate this conference is the one in which the British Prime Minister is so intensely interested: the new Europe of the Nine and its impact on the rest of the world. Every Commonwealth country is anxious about its relationship with this new economic giant and is looking to Britain for help in the long negotiations upon which each must embark this year and upon which will depend, in some cases, its whole economic future perhaps for decades to come. Mr Heath has firmly set his representatives in Brussels the task of pressing the EEC to become more outward-looking. Britain has more intimate relations with a larger part of the developing world than any of the other eight and her Prime Minister should welcome the opportunity Ottawa presents to make known his views to so many friends and to hear at first hand of the hopes and anxieties of the other thirty-one Commonwealth countries. Now that Britain is in the Common Market her Commonwealth connections can only enhance the British voice at Brussels and assist Mr Heath's hopes of a more outward-looking Community. Furthermore, Britain needs to prove to the Commonwealth that its arguments about British entry strengthening and not weakening the association were not empty and facile phrases.

There is a line in Whitehall, which could well emanate from No 10, that Heads of Government conferences are overrated in value and that the Commonwealth is much more effective working quietly away with day-to-day functional co-operation. It is true that the type of comment these meetings have recently attracted do not always help the image of the Commonwealth, but to talk down their importance is to imply that for thirty-two Presidents and Prime Ministers to get to know each other personally is not a useful exercise. Yet anyone who attends a conference or convention in any field knows that what takes place in the meeting room may be the least important aspect of the gathering. It is the personal relationships struck up in hotel suites and conference hall corridors that are of vital importance. Trudeau's friendship with such figures as Lee Kuan Yew and Julius Nyerere, first made in London in 1969 just after he became Prime Minister, has no doubt influenced his thinking considerably since then. Many other such examples could be quoted, and the effect of these encounters on subsequent trends in international relationships can be traced.

There are eight new Commonwealth Heads of Government since Singapore, and Ottawa gives them the opportunity to meet their opposite numbers that would only otherwise arise as a result of extensive travel over a number of years. The eight are: Colonel I. K. Acheampong (Ghana), General Idi Amin (Uganda), Norman Kirk (New Zealand), Michael Manley (Jamaica), Dom Mintoff (Malta), Lynden Pindling (Bahamas), Sheikh Mujibur Rahman (Bangladesh) and Gough Whitlam (Australia). Nearly all of these are likely to be present* and, in addition, there is the strong possibility that General Gowon will attend for the first time.

Summit meetings are bound to attract world public attention: they are the glamorous part of Commonwealth activities. But they also achieve much more than Whitehall in its current mood is prepared to accept. That they do not always achieve what Britain wants them to achieve may be true, but for some time now they have not been held just for Britain's benefit.

One of the major themes at Ottawa, arising out of British membership of the EEC, is expected to be the way in which the growing pattern of regional groupings fits into the pattern of international co-operation. As such organizations as the EEC, CARIFTA, ASEAN, the OAU and the OAS strengthen in character, one task of the world organizations, the United Nations and the Commonwealth, is to try to ensure that regionalism does not create groupings acting parochially and independently of each other in a manner that could create its own tensions. The business of the Commonwealth is to maintain and create links between continents.

Another debate will be on the Trudeau item Comparative Techniques of Government, which was squeezed out at Singapore and which was discussed by Commonwealth officials of Cabinet Secretary rank at the meeting in Ottawa last October. The October talks were so successful that further such meetings of civil servants are likely to take place in future years, and one idea which may be floated in August is that of the establishment of a study college which top Commonwealth civil servants would attend on courses lasting several months. Mr Trudeau is convinced that civil servants of Commonwealth countries have a great deal to learn from each other and that the experience of the newer countries might in many cases be of value to the old Commonwealth countries and might lead to the reinvigoration of systems that may have become too set in their ways.

The conference will put the seal on a major programme of youth service on a Commonwealth scale—the product of three years of study and several seminars held in countries of every continent and culminating in the Commonwealth conference on Youth held in Lusaka, Zambia, at the end of January. The result will be a wide-ranging programme of interchange and experience involving young people all over the Commonwealth. Other subjects the conference

* Acheampong and Amin did not attend.

will discuss are likely to include Indo-China, the Middle East, pollution, education, monetary reform and the progress of the Commonwealth Fund for Technical Co-operation (CFTC). The Fund has completed fifty projects and is now handling 100 more. It has been extended to include such matters as help for countries needing market research and advice on developing export markets.

In the past the conference has not discussed the date for the following summit meeting. This time attempts will be made to agree on a target period during which the next conference would be held. This will be arranged on the basis of a two-yearly meeting and would avoid the complications of negotiating between thirty-two governments at a late stage to find a mutually agreeable date.

Despite the welter of misunderstanding about the nature of the Commonwealth today, the downright hostility of a few vocal journalists and academics, and the indifference through ignorance of a great number of people, the Commonwealth is moving ahead. Many who have shown an almost unnatural antagonism to the Commonwealth concept and others who have become Doubting Thomases did not believe the Commonwealth would get thus far. Busy Presidents and Prime Ministers do not give up valuable time and travel halfway round the world unless they believe the effort worthwhile and this alone proves there is a durability in the Commonwealth association which many observers remain for the moment obstinately unwilling to recognize.

The Ottawa meeting did indeed open a new era which has been maintained. This was my report afterwards:

My favourite moment of the 1973 Commonwealth conference came on the last morning when the Heads of Government finally reached host Prime Minister Pierre Trudeau's pet item—Comparative Techniques of Government. The talk turned to the role of civil servants and how they can be kept effective, at the same time ensuring that ministers are not reduced to being rubber stamps. Then someone raised the problems of getting rid of civil servants. At that moment there came a bang—and some consternation. A senior civil servant had fallen off his chair. The conference being in private, we were not told afterwards whether he was re-crossing his legs or had simply dozed off. But I hope the poor fellow has not lost his job.

The importance of the Ottawa conference was its businesslike performance and its good humour throughout. For instance, President Nyerere had quoted in his opening remarks on the first day a Swahili saying that when the elephants fight it is the grass that suffers. He was referring to the détente between the superpowers, and the grass in this case was represented by the medium and small powers, which the Commonwealth comprises.

Premier Lee Kuan Yew saw it differently. He said it had occurred to him that when elephants flirt the grass also suffers, and when they make love it is disastrous. The Africans, who have rather more experience of observing elephants in love than most round the table, fell about with laughter. But they saw Lee's point. He was saying that Singapore's situation had actually become more difficult because of détente and that the same might apply to some other countries.

The atmosphere of friendliness and understanding of this conference moved General Gowon to coin the phrase 'The Spirit of Ottawa'. Only on the last day but one did a hint of old bitternesses return. Inevitably, the subject was Rhodesia. Premier Errol Barrow came into the room late from lunch waving a piece of paper to catch chairman Trudeau's eye. He had ripped off the news teleprinter in the lounge outside a report of burning of African villages by Rhodesian troops.

With emotion he said that while they sat talking, appalling events were going on in southern Africa and he rounded on Britain as the responsible power in Rhodesia. It happened that for almost the first time Mr Barrow's neighbour at the table, Premier Edward Heath of Britain, was not present. Nor was Dr Nyerere. When first one and then the other returned to the room, each helped to cool things down.

The significance of Rhodesia and Ottawa is that attempts at collective, constructive work by the Commonwealth on a solution have not hitherto been possible. They are a product of 'The Ottawa Spirit'. Never before, said one official who has attended several Commonwealth summit conferences in different capacities, have the British and the Africans seemed so close together.

If this was true of Rhodesia it was true of most other subjects—and this time no one topic dominated the conference. Less than a day was devoted to southern Africa. 'We all learned a lesson at Singapore', said Dr Nyerere, who is better at making frank admissions than most politicians.

Mr Heath learned at Singapore and at Ottawa, but he finds it more difficult to say so. The reluctant way in which Heath came to Ottawa is now almost political legend. He did not want a Commonwealth conference at any time this year; he did not really want to see another one for two or three years. He was frustrated to find that Britain could no longer in effect veto the holding of a conference—a symptom of Britain's totally changed position in the Commonwealth on which he has since commented not unfavourably.

When the date conflicted with Mr Heath's sailing plans the prospect of the meeting was even more irritating to him. He would not decide whether to attend until three weeks beforehand, but having gone to Ottawa he threw himself into it. As the days passed delegates watched with fascination the way the British Prime Minister relaxed. He went away saying he had enjoyed himself, and plainly he had.

He was thoroughly conscientious, sitting at the table the entire time, except for one brief absence, until he left Ottawa. When he departed one day early, no one could say he was cutting the conference. Yet until the second week he had stubbornly refused to declare how long he would stay and his plane was on standby. It was almost as if he was saying, 'If you boys behave yourselves I'll stay, otherwise I'm off'.

It was not a commendable attitude for any Commonwealth head of government to take up nor a generous one to host Trudeau. Mr Heath seemed to be under the mistaken impression that several others would not sit it out. But in fact only the Malaysian Prime Minister departed abruptly, and that was because his Deputy Premier had died suddenly, in Kuala Lumpur. Premier Michael Manley of Jamaica went off for twenty-four hours to attend his national day celebrations in Kingston, but all other heads of government stayed throughout.

However, it must be said that in the end Mr Heath played an impressive role and contributed much to the success of the conference, though he was not the 'star' as The Times suggested.

There were no 'stars', no victories, no defeats. This is not what a Commonwealth conference is about, and these meetings will only become fully valuable when Presidents and Prime Ministers stop trying to use their role for domestic political purposes. At Ottawa there was a marked change for the better. The message is getting through. There was much less playing to the gallery, though it still did happen from time to time.

If there were no 'stars' there were several outstanding performances. One was by Norman Kirk.* He is a fine addition to 'the club'. He made an impact right from the outset, first with a move to get a conference statement on nuclear testing, and then in many commonsense observations on subjects right through the agenda. Dr Nyerere and Mr Lee, veterans now—in the absence of President Makarios of Cyprus, Dr Nyerere was the longest-serving head of government present and therefore the Commonwealth doyen at Ottawa—kept their colleagues stimulated. Dr Nyerere's main speech on southern Africa enthralled the delegates just as his speeches had done in London in 1969 and in Singapore in 1971. Mr Lee was always maddeningly pragmatic (and overshadowed Malaysia's contribution in the absence of Tun Razak).

Two other newcomers made real impact. Mr Manley's speech on the problems of the ever-widening rich-poor gap was probably one of the two or three most valuable contributions of the entire conference. His simple illustrations included one to the effect that if the recommendation of the 1969 Lester Pearson Commission on aid—that all developed countries contribute one per cent of their GNP—was fully implemented, the poorer countries would still only reach a growth rate of about $12 a year per person compared with a current growth rate in North America of $180 a year.

Another was that if ten years ago you could buy a tractor with ten tons of sugar, today's tractor costs 50 tons of sugar. Yet there is no more land for sugar-growing in the Caribbean, and sugar technology has improved output little. 'So,' he said, 'it is with cotton from Tanzania or sisal. We're all trapped in this thing. It's almost like walking up the down escalator.'

The other impressive newcomer was General Gowon, who seemed to win over everyone with sheer charm and sincerity. He played a full part throughout and put many constructive ideas. He was important in the Rhodesia debate. The British, who these days find General Gowon just to their liking, seem to see differences between the views of General Gowon and Dr Nyerere on such issues as southern Africa.

But the difference is really in temperament, not in basic outlook. It has been said that Dr Nyerere could not order a boiled egg for breakfast without emotion, and that is probably true. It is partly

* This was Kirk's only Commonwealth conference. He died on 31 August 1974.

his emotional make-up that makes him such an attractive personality, quite aside from the wisdom of many of his remarks. General Gowon is not an emotional person, so he may sound to some ears more reasonable. The British will be mistaken if they think that as chairman of the Organization of African Unity, he will differ from Dr Nyerere in any fundamental way.

But General Gowon must take a minus for his pronouncement at Ottawa on General Amin's expulsion of the Asians. He said at a press conference: 'This is an internal matter. Amin had a problem, and I suppose it's the only way that he could solve it. . . . I'm not being unkind to these people, but I certainly would not like to accuse General Amin as being a racialist.'

I prefer what Dr Nyerere said: 'Racism is racism whoever practices it. The Asians in East Africa are pawns of racial cynicism.'

As always after a Commonwealth summit conference—and with most international conferences for that matter—people say: 'Yes, it's all very well, but what was actually *achieved*? What did they *decide*?' The best retort to that kind of remark to be given publicly during the conference came from Mr Heath. He said, 'It is accepted that Commonwealth summits are not occasions for making policies or decisions on the big issues. They are an opportunity to exchange ideas and to influence each other and this is reflected in policies.'

Mr Trudeau tackled the point at his final press conference. He told journalists, 'You people deal with words and obviously you think that words are important and that in the exchange of ideas they are important, otherwise you wouldn't write columns or editorials. . . . Academics spend half their time going to conferences or talking to each other and convincing each other that certain things are important. If it is true for them it is certainly more true for Heads of Government . . .'

The new procedures paid off handsomely.

Not all the texts disappeared and not everyone spoke briefly, but far fewer leaders brought prepared speeches and those who spoke at some length—President Nyerere on Rhodesia, for instance—were so good that their colleagues wanted to listen to every word. There was more of the atmosphere of a lively parliamentary debate, with points being picked up and queried as the discussion proceeded.

If there was criticism this time about the mode of procedure it was to the effect that so much care had been taken by Mr Trudeau and others to ensure a smooth conference that there could be a danger of inducing in the proceedings a state of such calm and equanimity that the whole exercise would be rendered meaningless.

This was not the case at Ottawa, where a greater variety of subjects was tackled than perhaps at any Commonwealth conference for more than a decade.

The detailed discussion that was held on trade and aid matters, coming after British entry into the EEC and on the eve of the long negotiations on EEC association in Brussels and the GATT negotiations, must have been valuable to almost every country. So was the major airing given to anxieties in developed as well as developing countries about the activities of multi-national companies. The decision to set up within the Commonwealth Fund for Technical Co-operation a section that would dig out the real facts about the widening gap between the rich and poor so that countries can work on realities was a real advance.

And then there were the nuts and bolts of Commonwealth on which the committee of officials worked hard while the Heads of Government were sitting. These included full backing for the Commonwealth Youth Programme launched in Lusaka a few months ago, and giving another £100,000 for the Commonwealth Foundation.

When to these matters is added the increased harmony on Rhodesia, the statement on nuclear testing, and the discussions that took place on subjects like rising food prices, increasing freight rates and the world's confused monetary situation, it represents a formidable body of work.

In the new relaxed Commonwealth atmosphere the thirty-two were able to bandy risqué remarks at each other all the time and no one took offence. When Mr Barrow of tiny Barbados, cracked at General Gowon 'It's all right for you—you've got a huge army to keep things in order while you're away, I've got nothing' Gowon just took it with his large engaging, twinkling laugh. Sometimes there were abrasive exchanges between Mr Lee and Mr Whitlam and between Mr Heath and Mr Whitlam, but the Australian Premier's views on multinational companies and foreign exploitation of a country's resources registered.

It was the emergence of unexpected themes like that of the activities of the multinationals that made the conference so worthwhile. A depth of feeling about the multinationals was revealed that probably Heath and Lee had not fully realized existed. Here was a subject that involved not just the developing countries that feel exploited but the developed like Australia and Canada, with Japanese, British and American companies entrenched; decisions taken in the US about the future of plants like Fords can affect the economic well-being of a whole area of Britain. General Gowon called attention to a different aspect of multinationals: the dangers they present to a country's security. Some, he pointed out, backed Biafra.

And what was in the Ottawa conference for Canada, as host? Certainly a nice calculation of risks and rewards. There were three main risks. The most important was that a gathering of thirty-two heads of Government—and even more of 800 accredited journalists—would attract a terrorist group like the Black September organization. The second was that the conference itself would produce ugly tensions, and Ottawa would be remembered as the burial ground of the Commonwealth.

The third risk was that Canadians, suffering already from sharp inflation, would take unkindly to the expenditure of several million dollars in staging the conference. There was a big bill to pay after Expo 67, and another is coming up with the 1976 Olympics in Montreal.

But Mr Trudeau escaped all these hazards. Well-organized (and well-publicized) security measures deterred any possible kidnappers or killers who might have come from overseas. As for any violence from Canadians, the Zambian foreign minister, who might have expected some demonstrators protesting about the shooting of the two girls at Victoria Falls, said he had not encountered a single unfriendly person.

The conference had its moments of rising temperature, if not temper, it is true. But Mr Trudeau at the end, received many plaudits as chairman, and saw as the clearest index of success the fact that several countries were 'vying for the responsibility' of running the 1975 Commonwealth conference.

The taxpayers did not seem to mind paying for the party. Getting the Queen (of Canada) at the same time meant the Anglo-Saxon Tories, who might have studied the bill critically, refrained from what might have been taken as an act of *lèse-majesté*.

So for Pierre Trudeau the rose never wilted, and the conference was all pure reward. For the price of a generous contribution to the Commonwealth Youth Programme and a larger grant to the Fund for Technical Co-operation, Canada showed it was in earnest about functional co-operation among the thirty-two member countries. As chairman Mr Trudeau was expected to find compromises. When he said less than he might have done on New Zealand's side on the issue of nuclear testing (for many Canadians were very angry, some months ago, with the Americans for threatening British Columbia with their underground test at Amchitka in the Aleutians), it was accepted that he was keeping to the middle of the road so that Britain would not be isolated at the outset of the conference.

On southern Africa, Mr Trudeau took a further step towards what the Canadian foreign policy papers of 1970 define as 'social justice'. He made it clear, at his final briefing conference, that he was opening up his options, and that Canada might before long be taking the line of the Scandinavian countries in helping Africans in the liberated areas with humanitarian aid.

There was speculation that, while making sure Britain hung in with the Commonwealth, young Canada was keen to take over its leadership from the mother country. With more decorum (and conviction) than Julius Caesar, Pierre Trudeau refused the crown. 'There is no leader,' he said—and meant it fervently.

CHAPTER EIGHT

Kingston 1975: Towards a New Order

At the Heads of Government meeting held in Jamaica 29 April–6 May 1975 the Commonwealth turned its attention to the whole question of the disparity in living standards between the developed and developing world. A Commonwealth now confident of its survival and usefulness began to look outside its own confines and to embark on an additional role—that of a complementary body helping other regional and international organisations and agencies.

A few months after the Ottawa conference had come the Yom Kippur war and what was to become known loosely as the 'oil crisis'. This, coupled with the world recession, precipitated the Third World's call for a New International Economic Order.

The Commonwealth began to focus on the state of the world's economy and ways in which there might begin to be a transfer of wealth from the rich to the poor nations. Michael Manley, the Prime Minister of Jamaica and therefore chairman of the Kingston meeting, and his Commonwealth Caribbean colleagues felt convinced that this subject should be the central theme of the conference—and it became so. This first report was written on the eve of the conference . . .

THE LEADERS OF thirty-three countries will sit round a new oval-shaped table in the Grand Jamaican Suite of Kingston's Pegasus Hotel on 29 April in a mood to take action on a subject that concerns every one of their 1,000 million peoples. They will be seeking to sow seeds in the search for a new world economic order. It is a high ideal, but in the eight days of their meeting Commonwealth Heads of Government hope to outline proposals that can be launched in other world fora as their contribution to the pressing problems that have been highlighted by the oil crisis.

In Jamaica the leaders are determined to make the Commonwealth a launching pad for new ideas and they want to go away with a feeling of achievement. There is a good chance of this happening, though the results will hardly be spectacular in headline terms. The Commonwealth has now moved into a constructive, quieter atmosphere—witness the almost total lack of speculation about the conference in the weeks leading up to this meeting.

At Ottawa much of the time was taken up with economic affairs; since then the Middle East October War of that year and the economic upheaval that flowed from it have led Commonwealth countries to a greater preoccupation than ever with the state of the world economy. It follows that this summit will be mostly about economic matters.

Governments are seeing the Commonwealth today as a grouping of medium and small countries, having no super-power, that contains within it most of the world's problems—and this applies particularly to matters of economic survival. Most Commonwealth countries are poor and deeply concerned about how the world's wealth can be redistributed to bring their people a better living.

Inflation will be in the forefront of everyone's minds at Kingston. It is a disease of the rich countries yet it has inevitably been exported to the poor ones and they find themselves suffering too. At Ottawa in 1973 Jamaican Prime Minister Michael Manley painted a grim picture of the plight of the developing countries and called for a scheme of indexation which would automatically link the prices of goods imported from the rich with the prices of goods exported by the poor.

Since then the United Nationals General Assembly has initiated several studies of the problem. As Manley has put it: 'The oil price phenomenon has forced a large part of the world to understand what an externally imposed inflation is like'.

Recognition has come with the Lomé Convention signed between the forty-six African, Caribbean and Pacific countries (ACP) and the European Economic Community. The EEC agreed to fund a scheme for the stabilization of export receipts covering a number of important products. It is called STABEX and it goes some way towards indexation.

These are highly complex economic matters but vital ones, and the Kingston conference will spend much time on them. And there are bound to be differences in methods of approach. The rich countries are against indexation.

The Kingston meeting will follow up the successful Commonwealth conference on Food and Rural Development held in London last March as a sequel to the United Nations Food Conference in Rome. Proposals agreed in London and put up to the Kingston conference—one is to set up at once a Food Production and Rural Development Division of the Commonwealth Secretariat—are likely to be given the green light. The subject of producers' cartels will be much to the fore. Interest will centre on proposals the British are expected to make. James Callaghan, Britain's Foreign and Commonwealth Secretary, told MPs recently that better machinery was needed for ending the situation that kept the industrialized nations rich and the developing countries poor.

He said: 'If we and the Commonwealth can secure some broad measure of agreement on the way to handle these problems, this would have an influence on the policies of the EEC, of OPEC, of the Group of 77 and the general attitude of the United Nations. This is one way in which the Commonwealth has a particular value and in which we can use it as an instrument of world policy.'

Callaghan referred specifically to machinery for dealing with raw materials and here the question of producers' cartels will come up, and probably produce argument. British Prime Minister Harold Wilson, speaking in the odd context of a dinner of the Leeds Branch of the Labour Friends of Israel, some weeks ago, attacked the development of cartel-like arrangements for commodity producers. He hinted that he would put forward at Kingston a plan for international price stabilization that would be in return for assurances from the producers that they do not persist in cartel arrangements.

Away from the economic field there will be much other business at Kingston. The Southern African debate may lack the old Commonwealth fireworks, but with the situation over Rhodesia changing almost daily, the conference will be eager to hear

Presidents Kaunda, Nyerere and Sir Seretse Khama report on the dramatic developments of the past months.* Mr Vorster and Mr Smith will be watching Kingston with interest from afar off.

Action will be taken at Kingston to help Namibia. A plan to train Namibians along the lines of the successful Commonwealth programme for Rhodesian Africans will be launched. Discussions have already taken place at the Commonwealth Secretariat with Sean McBride, the UN Commissioner for Namibia. Matters of Commonwealth precedent are involved here: Namibia is not an ex-British colony and until an independent government is formed there it cannot be known whether Namibia will join the Commonwealth. The indications are that an independent Namibia would join and no objections are likely to be put to helping Namibians now.

Then there is the Commonwealth's own domestic business—reviews of the programmes of co-operation; ways of increasing the size and scope of the Commonwealth Fund for Technical Co-operation; a renewal of mandate for the Commonwealth Foundation (which next year will be ten years old); and the choice of the new Secretary-General. There is only one candidate in the field to follow the retiring Arnold Smith: Shridath Ramphal, the Foreign Minister of Guyana. He is likely to be confirmed in the post at the end of the meeting and will take over at Marlborough House on 1 July.

Finally, there will also be discussion at Kingston of a new topic—the brain drain, a peculiarly Commonwealth disease which hits developed and developing countries alike—and another session in which President and Prime Ministers let their hair down and discuss how they run their governments, the item Comparative Techniques of Government. Being a head of government can be lonely and Commonwealth leaders like the chance to chat with their equals about their domestic problems. It's partly what the Commonwealth is all about.

---

* After the Portuguese coup of 25 April 1974 Mozambique had begun to move swiftly to independence. Following a long series of exchanges between Vorster and Kaunda pressure on Smith led to the release from detention of the Rhodesian nationalist leaders Joshua Nkomo and Rev Ndabaningi Sithole. Prolonged attempts followed to get the rival nationalist groups to unite. Bishop Muzorewa, leader of the African National Council, Nkomo and Sithole and other leaders came to Kingston during the conference and Muzorewa addressed the meeting. Soon afterwards the Victoria Falls meeting on the bridge with Smith took place. The talks collapsed after a few hours.

As expected the conference was not a headline-maker, but it did consolidate the Ottawa success and confirmed that the Commonwealth was now firmly set on its new course. This was the result . . .

No Commonwealth summit conference has been more compact than the one at Kingston. In three large hotels within 200 or 300 yards of each other stayed all the thirty-three delegations, and in the divided-up 'Grand Jamaica Suite' of one of them, the Pegasus, was held the meeting. No delegate needed to take a car to visit another; he could just walk across. Even on the morning of the formal opening, several Presidents and Prime Ministers went on foot to the foyer of the Pegasus where Manley and Arnold Smith were waiting to receive them.

A small knot of people stood at the entrance (security round the whole compound kept the numbers low). President Nyerere of Tanzania was a particular favourite when he arrived—people cried out 'Rainmaker', a reference to the fact that on his previous visit to Jamaica rain had fallen and ended a drought.

The containment of all the delegations in a small area contributed to the generally intimate atmosphere of the entire gathering. Probably never before at a Commonwealth conference have so many officials been in such close and frequent contact with one another.

The Jamaicans did a fine organizational job that was totally free of hitches. Even the efficient Canadians, at Ottawa in 1973, slipped up in transporting delegates for the weekend at Mont Tremblant and found themselves having to smooth the tempers of at least one delegation. No such problem occurred in moving everyone to Tryall, at the other end of the island, where Presidents and Prime Ministers, perhaps slightly incongruously, were able to talk informally about such matters as the new world economic order in dream villas that cost ordinary folk not like you and me £900 a week to rent. ('For less than you could imagine,' says the brochure of the Tryall Golf and Beach Club, 'you can enjoy an air-conditioned home of your own. . . .')

In true Caribbean style it was 'all right on the night'—even though a week or two before it had not seemed possible that everything would be ready on time. One late anxiety was the actual table round which delegates sat. It had originally been intended to have it made from Guyanese wood. But first it was discovered that, if everyone was to be seated comfortably, such a table would not fit into the space allocated. Then the wood was not available in time. So the order for an oval table was given late to a furniture maker in Kingston, who rushed the huge job through in a few weeks. In the end everything was attended to, even the specially large chair required for the Tongan Prime Minister.

So to the conference itself. The turnout of Presidents and Prime Ministers was higher than ever before. Only five of the thirty-three were absent (Kenyatta of Kenya, Acheampong of Ghana, Amin of Uganda, Williams of Trinidad, Banda of Malawi). All the indications are that no one went home disappointed, though not unnaturally some were happier than others. Mrs Gandhi, who until a couple of weeks before had been undecided about attending (she missed Singapore and Ottawa), was said to be well satisfied with the meeting.

Mr Trudeau had a not entirely happy meeting; a major irritant was that he was seated beside Mr Harold Wilson who enveloped the Canadian Prime Minister in clouds of smoke from his pipe for much of each day. It may seem a minor matter, but of such small personal whims and fancies history is made. Mr Trudeau also became agitated on the second day because his colleagues showed signs of drifting back to the habit of making long speeches, a feature he had successfully eliminated as Chairman at Ottawa in 1973.

Mr Lee Kuan Yew (who was decidedly off form at Kingston, and in any case should have known better since he was the victim of the long-speeches-and-texts disaster at Singapore in 1971) set a bad example by speaking for one hour and forty minutes when he opened the debate on international affairs on the second day. Mr Trudeau strongly holds to the view—and all Commonwealth countries have agreed—that this conference must consist of an exchange of views across the table, with brief interventions, and not long speeches.

After the second day, the Canadians began to make their displeasure known among delegations and it was then agreed to institute a rule that no one should speak longer than ten minutes. When Manley introduced this rule after Mr Dom Mintoff had been talking for half-an-hour, the Prime Minister of Malta said, 'Does my ten minutes start from now?' Manley gave him the benefit of the doubt, and Lee cracked across the table, 'Now we know why you are such a successful bargainer.'

In many ways this was a much more loosely structured and fluid conference than any other in recent years, and that turned out to be no bad thing. The agenda was not worked through rigidly item by item. Instead one item was discussed, dropped, and picked up again, which meant that, for example, the economic and political discussions merged at points instead of being contained within watertight compartments.

The room used for all the sessions except that of the formal opening, was modelled on the one at Ottawa, fitted on one side with a series of portable glass boxes, in which sat the note-takers and other officials of the Secretariat. This meant, that, as before, only the Prime Ministers and Presidents with their two assistants behind them, sat in the room. Each of the thirty-three leaders had an amplifying microphone. In one corner, sat the secretary of the conference, Nigerian Mr Ameka Anyaoku, who is head of the International Affairs Division of the Secretariat, and his assistant.

At one session only Heads of Government were present, with the Secretary-General in attendance and no notes taken. This was the meeting devoted to Comparative Techniques of Government. Another session was declared informal—that addressed by Bishop Muzorewa.* This formula was arrived at so as not to set a precedent by which other outsiders could plead special causes at future Commonwealth conferences. For this meeting, delegates sat about informally—and Mr Trudeau moved away from his usual seat and sat at the back, well out of range of Mr Wilson's pipe.

For the first time the conference had a formal public opening with television cameras present. There were five speeches—those from Mr Manley, Prime Minister Mrs Gandhi of India, Secretary-General Arnold Smith, President Makarios of Cyprus and Prime Minister Rowling of New Zealand. Mr Manley's speech was eloquent and moving and set the tone for the whole conference. He said, 'As we discuss the tons of sugar or bales of cotton which buy a tractor, I insist that we remember the human beings who depend upon the exchange. A housewife in America or Europe may be annoyed by the price of her lumps of sugar, but the increment which irritates her may be saving the children of a million sugar workers from malnutrition if not starvation.'

The experiment of the public opening was a success. It in no way

---

* Leader of the African National Council (ANC) in Rhodesia.

detracted from the privacy and intimacy of the subsequent meetings, but it did serve a vital publicity purpose by affording people a chance to see on television more than just a few leaders shaking hands with their host as they walked into the conference room. The practice should be continued.

Two subjects weaved in and out of the eight days of discussion: attempts to move towards a new international economic order, and the situation in southern Africa. Manley put it well at the closing press conference. 'It has,' he said, 'been important for the future of the Commonwealth that we should have been able to grapple with these things without wrenching disagreement.'

Throughout the hours of talks the prevailing atmosphere was of a will to succeed on the two gut issues. Expected strong differences emerged between the developed and developing countries. There was a large body of centre opinion, with Britain lagging behind somewhat at one end of the philosophical spectrum, and the Caribbean and some African countries at the other.

On the New International Economic Order—a term Britain's Harold Wilson did not accept at first but which is now enshrined in the communiqué—the crunch came over the Caribbean proposal for a restructuring of the world's financial organizations such as the World Bank and the International Monetary Fund. Prime Minister Forbes Burnham of Guyana, presenting the Caribbean (and the developing world's) case, gave ground here and accepted the words 'reform and where necessary the restructuring', but on balance the Caribbean gave less ground than Wilson.

Right up to 4 p.m. on the last day Mr Manley and Mr Wilson, in a series of face-to-face meetings outside the conference, bargained with each other, with the Canadians, Australians and New Zealanders happy to go along with Mr Wilson as their unofficial leader. The moral attitude in the first five pages of Wilson's original speech went down well with the Caribbeans, but they found his six-point proposals on page six unexciting, even old fashioned.

Some said they went no further than the proposals he personally made when negotiating the Commonwealth Sugar Agreement in 1951. The action decided on by the conference is the setting up of a Commonwealth Experts Group of ten to work out ideas on how progress can be made towards a new economic order. The Chairman will be Mr Alister McIntyre, who is Secretary-General of the

Caribbean Community (CARICOM).

The Caribbean was so pleased at the concessions Mr Wilson made to them that Mr Burnham suggested a statement be issued separately to the effect that the Commonwealth supported Britain's membership of the EEC. No one dissented from this idea and some leaders, including Dr Nyerere of Tanzania, said British withdrawal from the Market would be positively harmful.

On Southern Africa the communiqué takes the Commonwealth on a tougher road than it has so far travelled. A reference to the illegal occupation of Namibia replaced the British-favoured word 'unlawful'. The British have also accepted without qualification the use of the African name Zimbabwe for Rhodesia. On the other hand, they have firmly set themselves against any commitment of arms and money for the freedom fighters.

The Africans want help in building their liberation army so that they can back the talking with Ian Smith by force. Dr Nyerere asked for money point blank but the British would not consider the idea. The Mozambique squeeze is one of the important decisions of the conference.

No time is being lost in implementing the pledge to back up that country with cash and technical aid when it closes its frontier to Rhodesian traffic. The Commonwealth Secretary-General sent a message to his UN counterpart Kurt Waldheim telling him of the conference decision.

The presence of the African nationalist leaders in Kingston led to exhaustive discussion of the Rhodesian problem outside the conference room. The British were pressed but not confronted with demands for more action, especially for the calling of a constitutional conference.

For Namibia there is now a firm invitation to join the Commonwealth as a full member when it becomes independent. A new squeeze is to be put on arms supplies to South Africa, and the Commonwealth is to step up the training of Africans from Zimbabwe and Namibia.

If there was a star at Kingston it was Mr Manley, who conducted the chairmanship in a way that many observers thought more impressive than any of his predecessors. The manner in which he picked up points made and proceeded to get them developed round the table was much admired. So was the way, every now and again, he summed up what he saw as the consensus view—something no previous chairman had attempted. Apart from his natural personal charm, Mr Manley showed throughout all his public performances and at the press conferences fluency and grasp of subject.

Mrs Gandhi was respected for a quiet and dignified—and cogent—performance, and there was high regard for the newcomer Mr Wallace Rowling of New Zealand. He faced the difficult task of following the late Mr Norman Kirk, who had made such a personal impact at Ottawa. President Nyerere, as always, compelled attention with his directness and humour and Mr Burnham commanded more attention than he has ever done at a Commonwealth conference.

Mr Wilson won regard, if not always agreement, for his performance in the economic debates, but how much better it would have been if the Burnham and Wilson papers had been circulated some weeks before the conference through the Secretariat so that the leaders had had a chance to absorb the arguments in advance of arriving at the table. Both could then simply have talked to their papers and more time would have been available for nitty-gritty discussion.

Here again, we come back to the politicians' hankering for personal publicity. Mr Wilson had given notice months earlier that he was planning to make a big economic initiative at Kingston. In the days before the debate opened, the British were building up for the launching—'the most important economic initiative since World War II', some dubbed it.

A twenty-four-page memorandum with a much longer appendix and charts and diagrams was distributed to delegations only twenty-four hours before Wilson spoke and his actual speech was read by a mere handful of people before he delivered it. (Burnham and Manley were given a copy the night before and burned some midnight oil revising the Burnham speech.)

The British, it seems, have still not learned the Trudeau rules for Commonwealth conferences, even though they agree with them. They really must give up ideas about trying to play Commonwealth conferences for the voters back home. The point will need to be fully taken on board before the next meeting in London, where the temptation for the British will be very great, otherwise the progress made in recent years towards moving the Commonwealth away from the old Anglocentricity could be set back.

Kingston was not all sweetness and light. The conference produced no confrontation but there were rough moments. The British attacked the newest member, Grenada, for allegedly misappropriating funds from the Government. Wilson quoted Kipling to support an argument against sending a force to guarantee the independence of Belize and there was the Trudeau annoyance at the number of long set speeches.

But it was, above all, a friendly conference. Dr Nyerere set the tone when he said at his press conference just after the meeting opened, 'We are not looking for fireworks.' There were not any; disappointing for the Press but good for the Commonwealth.

What we did find was a genuine Caribbean gaiety throughout. At the informal receptions held in the gardens of King's House, where the Governor-General lives, and Jamaica House, where the Prime Minister lives, half the population of the island seemed to have been invited. There were fashion shows and steel bands and dancing, with people like Mr Gough Whitlam and President Kenneth Kaunda lost in a sea of Commonwealth people.

Can there be any other international gathering at such a high level that generates so much genuine friendship and family feeling?

I certainly don't know of one.

*   *   *

The Commonwealth Experts Group went to work fast. They produced their first report* in time for the Commonwealth Finance Ministers' meeting in Georgetown, Guyana (26-8 August). Not everything in it was acceptable to the industrialized countries of the Commonwealth, but they let it go forward to the UN Seventh Special Session, which met the following month to discuss the New International Economic Order. It became a respected document and gained considerable attention among delegates. A second report was produced by the Group in time for the fourth meeting of the United Nations Conference on Trade and Development (UNCTAD Four) in Nairobi (May 1976). During this conference Commonwealth delegates held five meetings of their own.

By now it had become clear that the Third World was going to find the march towards the New International Economic Order a very long one. The industrialized countries had hardened their line towards the poor as the American presidential election grew closer. Britain's position moved some way back from the Kingston initiative taken by Mr Wilson. At Nairobi, much to the disappointment of the developing countries, Britain lined itself up with Japan, West Germany and the United States in resisting the

---

* Towards a New International Economic Order.

99

proposal for a conference to discuss the setting up of a Common Fund for commodities.

At the Commonwealth Finance Ministers' conference in Hong Kong in 1976 (30 September-1 October) Britain, by now deeper than ever in its own economic difficulties, showed no change of heart, except a readiness to accept a novel proposal that on certain demands the Commonwealth should have a single spokesman at the World Bank meeting which was to follow immediately in Manila, the Philippines. One such point was the urgent need to agree on the amount of the Fifth Replenishment of the International Development Association (IDA).

This was a significant development: never before had the Commonwealth let one of its number speak at an international meeting for all thirty-six nations. The Ministers chose the Canadian delegate. The move could be directly traced back to the stepping up of co-operation in the world economic debate initiated at the Kingston conference sixteen months before.

CHAPTER NINE

Co-operation: A Professional Success Story

One of the most successful programmes of Commonwealth co-operation in recent years has been that carried out by the Commonwealth Foundation, which was set up in 1966 to encourage the development of Commonwealth professional associations throughout the Commonwealth and to help individual professional people to further their careers by enabling them to attend specialist seminars and conferences they would not otherwise have any chance of reaching.

The Foundation is housed in Marlborough House, but it is quite separate from the Secretariat. Its trustees are representatives of Commonwealth countries and some others, including the Commonwealth Secretary-General. Its budget is small; it now receives £700,000 a year from thirty-five member governments. But its impact is quite remarkable, as is shown by the two reports which follow.

In 1971—just before the 'brink' summit conference—I was invited to attend a one-day conference at which the work of the Foundation was discussed. This was my report afterwards . . .

IT WAS THE doctor who made the most telling remark of the day. He looked across the Chairman, Ghanaian Robert Gardiner, and at thirty-odd colleagues and said: 'The group sitting round this table is probably making a better job of it than politicians.' The men and women at that same long table that had been used for several Commonwealth Prime Ministers' meetings were a rather distinguished bunch.

They included one or more architects, lawyers, magistrates, pharmacists, town planners, geographers, engineers, nurses, chartered accountants, librarians, and a few others beside. They had been gathered together for a day for the first time by the Commonwealth Foundation in Marlborough House, London, to tell each other about their work in building up Commonwealth-wide co-operation.

Here, in this room, was proof that the Commonwealth was alive as a conception, for these men and women represented tens of thousands of professional people who were increasingly banding together to improve the quality of their work—service to the public of thirty-one countries. Much that was represented in that room is new in the last few years. The Foundation itself is new, founded in 1966, by Commonwealth Governments, funded by twenty-six of them to the extent of only £250,000 a year, directed by ex-diplomat John Chadwick with a tiny staff.*

The Foundation's job is to help the peoples of the Commonwealth to share the backgrounds, experience and skills of their professional people. Its money is disbursed to prime pumps, to act as a pacemaker to make it easier for professional people to meet and to build up a better chain of liaison than exists so far.

What was remarkable about the meeting was that it soon became plain that although there would seem to be little in common between librarians and pharmacists or between magistrates and town planners in fact a common set of aims and needs applied to them all.

Sir Thomas Lund, of the International Bar Association, set out those aims clearly in three categories:

1. To improve the standard of service to the public.
2. To enhance the status of our profession.
3. To educate and train the rising generation.

Sir Thomas was at the meeting as an observer, sitting with the Secretary of the Commonwealth Legal Bureau. His own

* Three at the outset and nine now.

association is world-embracing and yet he admitted: 'I find it much easier at a Commonwealth gathering to get along.'

The meeting was a down-to-earth test of the Commonwealth argument: Is it myth or reality? For these professional men are not given to wasting their time on non-starters. In the middle of the discussion Mr Gardiner broke in to force the delegates to face up to the question squarely: 'Do we see a role for the Commonwealth, or now we have got here do we say: "We have no need for it"?' The answer from right round the table was in no doubt, for delegates had proved already by their record of action that there was a need.

Several of the organizations represented had come into being only recently. This is the roll call:

The *Commonwealth Magistrates Association* was formed at a meeting of magistrates from twenty-three countries in London in July 1970. The Foundation grant enabled many to attend. Tom Skyrme, who holds the post in Britain of Secretary of Commissions (which comes under the Lord Chancellor), is Chairman of the new Association which is to have its HQ in London for the first years.

The *Commonwealth Nurses Federation* is in the course of being formed. When the Congress of the International Council of Nurses took place in Montreal in 1970 nurses from thirty-five Commonwealth countries were there—many on grants from the Foundation. They held a separate meeting and agreed to plan a Commonwealth Federation to help increase personal contacts and methods of mutual help and support between each other.

The *Commonwealth Association of Planners* has sprung from a meeting of town planners of nineteen countries held in London in September 1970. The Town Planning Institute in London had told the Foundation of the need for such a Commonwealth association and the Foundation helped to finance the meeting. The new body will be following the example of the *Commonwealth Association of Surveying and Land Economy*, which has existed for only two years.

The *Commonwealth Pharmaceutical Association* came into being in January 1971. It followed a meeting of twenty-nine countries, and already it has held in Uganda a regional meeting of pharmacists. The Foundation has given it £30,000 for its first three years.

The *Commonwealth Veterinary Association*, the *Commonwealth Legal Bureau* and the *Commonwealth Geographical Bureau* are all only about two years old and the newest baby is a *Commonwealth Association of Institutes of Public Administration.*

The Foundation is bringing professional people together more frequently in several other ways. Most promising is the development of Commonwealth professional centres—that is small headquarters at which doctors and architects, magistrates and pharmacists might meet each other regularly, a place which can keep professional men in touch with the latest journals and information in their field. Such centres will be invaluable in the smaller countries where the professions do not have their own individual headquarters.

Already there are Centres in Kampala (Uganda), Port-of-Spain (Trinidad), Nairobi (Kenya) and Singapore. Others are being formed in Kingston (Jamaica), Malta and Bridgetown (Barbados). Another notable child of the Foundation is the setting up of a school for the training of teachers of the Deaf in Blantyre, Malawi—the first of its kind in East and Central Africa.

The whole Foundation operation is designed as a mutual effort in which peoples of all countries of the Commonwealth join, learning from each other. As one of the delegates said at Marlborough House: 'We would not think we've got all the knowledge—here in Britain we've made a lot of mistakes and perhaps others can make a better job of it.'

And another gave the complete answer to anyone who still had doubts whether there is a role for Commonwealth co-operation. He said: 'We must be filling a role. The very success that all of us have had would not have been possible if there had been a lack of enthusiasm. If we don't fill the vacuum somebody else will.'

Four years later, in January 1975, I was invited to take part in a seminar organized by the Foundation which was held in Kingston, Jamaica, under the abstruse title: The Professions, Universities and Civil Servants—Mutual Interaction. It turned out to be a much more interesting occasion than the title indicated. In the course of the meeting the whole philosophy behind the work of the Foundation came under examination and after it was over I wrote this report . . .

When a government draws up a national development plan, it has to seek the help of people in dozens of specialist fields—scientists, land surveyors, doctors, lawyers, statisticians and so forth. If an item in that plan is, say, a dam to generate power, large areas may have to be inundated in the process of building it. The land may have to be requisitioned and people re-housed. Experts in land settlement will be needed. So will lawyers. And doctors will have to advise on health arrangements for the displaced people. Thus in any such scheme not only civil servants will be involved; experts from universities and professionals of several disciplines must be called in too.

The other day a mixture of academics, professionals and civil servants from a dozen countries of the Commonwealth met in Kingston and talked about this interdependence.

There were thirty-six delegates—six from Britain, one from India, one from Singapore, one from New Zealand, one from Ghana, three from Canada, two from Australia and 21 from the Caribbean. They talked for a total of 24 hours spread over six days.

Now the delegates have returned to their home countries the question has to be asked: Was all the talking worthwhile and if it was, what did it achieve? Did this seminar, set up by the Commonwealth Foundation as part of its continuing exercise to help the professions in all Commonwealth countries to cross-fertilize among themselves and with universities and governments, do anything more than actually contribute words to yet another report that few people will have the time to digest?

To answer that question with a straight Yes or No would be to court a charge of, at best subjectivity and, at worst, dishonesty. But I do not believe that anyone gets anywhere by staying at home and keeping minds apart; there has to be, in the jargon of the day, continuing dialogue.

Jibes about international talking shops are easy to make, whether they refer to agencies of the United Nations, the Commonwealth, such bodies as the World Council of Churches or regional organizations like the Association of South East Asian Nations (ASEAN), the Organization of African Unity (OAU), or any of the Caribbean organizations. But they have to be dismissed because no one has yet come forward with any alternative to sorting out problems face to face and all these organizations help to do just that.

It followed that when you bring together thirty-six people of the calibre of men like Sir Egerton Richardson, Sir Hugh Springer, Sir George Cartland, A. L. (Yaw) Adu, and T. H. McCombs, points that are well worth considering are bound to emerge.

105

Sir Egerton is Permanent Secretary of Jamaica's Ministry of Public Service, Sir Hugh is Secretary-General of the Commonwealth Universities Association, Sir George is Vice-Chancellor of Tasmania University, Mr Adu was Ghana's No 1 civil servant and later Deputy Commonwealth Secretary-General, and Mr McCombs is former Chancellor of Christchurch University, New Zealand.

The seminar was on 'The Professions, Universities and Civil Servants—Mutual Interaction' and some would say that a certain amount of intellectual incestuousness, even preciousness, crept in from time to time. But crucial and live issues were worked over and important practical ideas that can affect all of us came out of the talks.

The seminar was held against the backdrop of what the final report will describe as 'an unremitting increase in the growth of knowledge and of a worldwide need to restructure national economies in the light of the oil crisis'.

Governments, universities, the professions and the business and financial sectors of the worldwide community have a growing duty to ensure that they co-operate increasingly in the national, regional and international interest.

The thirty-six accepted that governments all over the world would inevitably become more and more involved in our lives. But civil servants could no longer hope, unaided, to recommend solutions. Only by co-operating with experts at universities, professional people and leaders from the private sector could Governments take decisions based on the fullest understanding of the problems facing them and in the widest public interest.

So the seminar tried to find out what roles each could play to bring about this co-operation, taking fully into account that in Commonwealth countries the British heritage and conventions, admired as they might be, had not proved the most successful of transplants.

Governments, it was thought, ought to accept more than they do now that academics and professionals were equally concerned with national development and planning. They should be asked to help formulate policy at the earliest stage and be encouraged to provide expert and unbiased advice.

Delegates concluded that as man's store of knowledge grows and problems become increasingly complex the trend towards state involvement in our day-to-day living is seen all over the world and is by no means confined to developing countries. Thus academics and professionals should be asked to involve themselves in policy formulation affecting the public interest at the earliest stage and be encouraged to provide expert and unbiased advice.

But to do this could increase public distrust and suspicion of professionals and academics; already there is a gap between the general public and such people as doctors and lawyers and accountants who, many feel, have an influence and power over their lives and in society which they themselves cannot achieve. Therefore it was suggested that laymen should be increasingly brought into committees and councils involved with planning and decisions affecting the quality of life.

Dr John B. MacDonald, Executive Director of the Council of Ontario Universities, suggested up to fifty per cent lay membership of such bodies—a proposition which would almost certainly be heavily challenged by most medical and legal professional bodies for a start, though token moves in this direction have been made in some countries. Dr MacDonald said: 'A partnership of public and profession will aid both. The profession will gain the advantage of a better perception of public concerns and priorities than is the case when the profession is making unilateral decisions. Professions commonly profess bewilderment when their decisions, made with innocent conviction, result in public indignation. Conversely, the public too often has a simplistic view of the issues being dealt with by the professions and consequently unrealistic expectations about what is possible.'

The rapidly changing economic situation required much rethinking of current training, retraining and research programmes. Again universities and academics could help.

The professions, for their part, needed to take a fresh look at themselves and at acceptable standards of achievement. One of the most important suggestions to be made at the seminar was that laymen should be brought on to government and non-government committees and councils involved with planning and decisions affecting the quality of life.

Professional bodies should offer advice to government without waiting to be consulted. They needed to be less stand-offish. Professions and universities had to close the gap between themselves and the public; they must become less elitist and distant and they needed to go in for some effective public relations.

With the coming together of the public and private sectors civil servants should be exposed to business administration, particularly in the field of international finance. They could have on-the-job training with private business so that they were more competent to handle the increasing number of public corporations.

The professions ought to advise on the content of training for sub-professionals. Mid-career training programmes for high-level administrators, academics, professionals and business leaders needed to be stepped up.

Acceptable levels of achievement in professional fields had to be reviewed. In developing countries professionals tended to be too rigid in their demands for training standards, comparable with those in developed countries.

Walter A. Burke and Edwin W. Carrington, both of the Caribbean Community Secretariat, asked in their Paper whether it was worthwhile producing ten more doctors unless they were combined with say forty para-medicals? Did developing countries need more economists at the expense of perhaps a new programme in tourism and hotel management?

Professionals who worked on the physical environment, said Sir Egerton Richardson, should look at techniques in other developing countries. He instanced China, where, not having enough heavy equipment for major projects, the large machine had to be supplemented with the small machine, the small machine with hand labour. Large bull-dozers, heavy tractors, small tractors, wheelbarrows and men and women carrying earth in baskets were employed at the same time in the same project.

Sir Egerton acknowledged that the expertise of private enterprise was unlikely to be found already in the possession of public servants and so such experts would have to be brought into the public service. Employment conditions would have to be adjusted to accommodate them.

The universities, on the other hand, could not practically make a major contribution through the public service. Nor might it be desirable. Sir Egerton said: 'In any case the quality of national development in the long term is already theirs to determine, for with the growth of nationalism their influence on the choices and standards of higher education will be paramount.'

Messrs Burke and Carrington backed the point: with university education no longer being the prerogative of the privileged few, academics now came into contact with large sections of the population.

'They can accordingly also contribute to opinion—forming in

108

the indirect way through the regional influence they have on their students, who, after all, are part of individual national constituencies. There is therefore need for a continuing awareness of the goals of society as expressed through the state if the contribution which the universities have to make is to be constructive.

'This is no attempt to deny the universities their independence nor does one suggest that they should directly involve themselves in the affairs of the state. They can nevertheless not afford to remain outside the mainstream of national and regional life.'

The two-way channel between universities and governments could itself become an avenue by which government policies and plans might be beneficially influenced through inputs from the world of the academic. Many other problems were discussed during the seminar. The brain drain was one; the problem of how politically committed professionals should be, another.

The seminar had its failures. One was in not coming to grips with defining what is a professional. Robert Steel, secretary of the Commonwealth Association of Surveying and Land Economy, accepted the proposition that a profession had four characteristics: 1. That its terms of entry should be well defined; 2. That it imposed a discipline on its members; 3. That before a member of a profession can practise he may have to submit his qualifications to some statutory or authoritative body; and 4. That it holds itself out primarily to exercise its skills in the interest of others.

Successful as it has been, the Foundation's activities have by their very nature raised a number of broad issues that are of fundamental importance to professional people all over the Commonwealth (and, for that matter, outside the Commonwealth).

Is a professional simply a doctor or a lawyer or an accountant or a nurse—in other words, someone who has skills that most of us do not have and in whom we as laymen can (and must) put our unquestioning trust? Or do we include in that category those who also have specialist skills but who until now have not been regarded as professional people—say bankers or journalists? If we do not include such people then we may be encouraging the growth of an elitist group within society which consists only of the chosen few.

And then there is the position of the professional politically. The traditional view would be that a professional should remain wholly aloof from politics. He is the servant of the government whatever its complexion and having discussed and put his viewpoint he should then accept to carry out to the best of his professional ability what he has been charged to do.

But another view would be that in the highly political world of today this is quite unrealistic; that the professional cannot remain a man or a woman apart, and should even embrace a political philosophy and here the relationship between the civil servant, the professional and government comes into play.

CHAPTER TEN

The Queen and The Commonwealth: An Untold Story

Partly because the workings of the Commonwealth itself do not get much public attention and partly because the role of Head of the Commonwealth has at times been a delicate one, the personal part played by the Queen is little written about. The historic records, however, will in due course reveal a close involvement throughout the reign. This essay, written on the eve of the conference in Jamaica in 1975 and now brought up to date, raised a corner of the curtain and contained some hitherto unpublished facts about the Queen and the Commonwealth.

LOOKING BACK NEARLY a quarter of a century, how appropriate it was that Princess Elizabeth should have received news that she had become Queen while she was staying in Kenya—a Commonwealth country. It was as if history had put up a signpost, for in the quarter century since that event Queen Elizabeth's reign has been dominated historically by the demolition of Empire and construction of Commonwealth and by a personal and close relationship with the countries and leaders of the Commonwealth that has no parallel.

Not only is the Queen the most travelled monarch in history; she has also become perhaps better acquainted with more political leaders over a longer period of the Twentieth Century than almost any politician. And these leaders do not only include those in the developed world; she knows well an even larger number of leaders of the Third World.

The development of these relationships and the accumulation of international experience by a Queen over fifty years old is not something that has been generally appreciated or so far been much commented on. Largely this is because her overseas visits have inevitably become less newsworthy as the years have passed (the Duke once admitted candidly that the Queen and himself had become middle-aged and therefore less interesting) and usually seen only in isolation, while the total effect has been little considered.

The Queen's position as the monarch who reigned at the time of decolonization combined with the unique nature of the decolonization itself (the transformation of Empire into Commonwealth) means that her own personal position has been deeply and continuously constitutionally implicated. She has found herself becoming Queen of countries of the Third World like Jamaica, Fiji and Papua New Guinea (and earlier Ceylon and Nigeria and Malawi) after such countries had become totally independent states with no constitutional connection with Britain.

Even though a young woman in the Fifties, all this must have required a tremendous personal adjustment for one who had been brought up as the daughter of a King-Emperor and as the heiress to an imperial tradition deeply ingrained in the machinery of monarchy as it existed in 1952.

At the time Elizabeth became Queen only five years had elapsed since Indian independence. The Commonwealth consisted of just eight members—Britain, Canada, Australia, South Africa, New Zealand, India, Pakistan, and Ceylon, of which the last three

112

pointed to the future. African colonies were becoming restive but not startlingly so. Mau Mau had not come to Kenya (during that period Treetops Hotel, where the Queen had stayed, was destroyed). War against the Communists was raging in Malaya, but many other upheavals—Cyprus, Aden, Ghana, Central Africa—were yet to come.

The pattern for the Commonwealth of the future had already been set, first in 1947 with Indian independence and then with the formula (evolved with the help of the Queen's cousin, Earl Mountbatten) for George VI to take on the title Head of the Commonwealth and thus enabling republics to stay within the Commonwealth. Burma, which had become independent in 1947 had had to leave the Commonwealth because there was then no way in which it could constitutionally remain a member country. (If the Head-of-the-Commonwealth formula had been devized earlier Burma would probably today still be in the Commonwealth.)

In 1952 India and Pakistan were republics within the Commonwealth and Ceylon was a monarchy along with the five older members of the Commonwealth (only in 1972 did Ceylon—now Sri Lanka—become a republic). Today the Queen is monarch of only eleven of the thirty-six member countries of the Commonwealth. Twenty-one are republics and the other four, such as Malaysia, have their own national monarchichal systems.

The change in the whole scene, over twenty years, with grave political differences often arising between the former imperial power, of which she was Queen, and other members of the Commonwealth, of which she was Head, meant that the Queen was often personally involved in a way that required a rare and delicate diplomatic touch. The experience that the Queen built over the years is a factor of which it is now appropriate to take stock.

An interesting speculation is whether Commonwealth countries would have continued to accept the British monarch as Head of the Commonwealth if there had been two or three changes of monarch in the past twenty years, as in the Thirties. The chances are that there might well have been some restlessness among Third World members of the Commonwealth leading either to departures from the association or a request for a new formula under which the position of Head of the Commonwealth rotated in some way.

As it is, the Queen has been a constant factor throughout, and her relaxed personal relationship with Commonwealth presidents and prime ministers and with other statesmen has been all-important. The Queen and the Duke of Edinburgh, together with their advisers, have kept fully abreast of change in the Commonwealth in a way which some politicians—particularly many in Britain who ought to have known better—have not.

Unlike many of her British Ministers and at least one British Prime Minister, the Queen has never wavered in her view that a Commonwealth stripped of all imperial and neo-colonial overtones is a valuable association of nations worth preserving.

The Queen has thus taken, quietly and unobtrusively, a highly independent line as Head of the Commonwealth. She has, in the first instance, made more frequent and warmer and more constructive references to it in her speeches than any major British political leader has seen fit to do, while the Duke of Edinburgh has never ceased to express his faith in its ability to survive; one of his most famous quotes several years ago was that the Commonwealth will still be around long after 'we are all pushing up the daisies'.

At Christmas 1973 the Queen scored a minor triumph by weaving her television broadcast round the Ottawa Commonwealth conference, with informal shots of herself in discussion with such men as President Nyerere of Tanzania, Prime Minister Pierre Trudeau of Canada and Prime Minister Lee Kuan Yew of Singapore.

This was the conference Edward Heath had until the last minute been uncertain about attending and even on arrival would not commit himself to staying longer than the first few days.

The Queen had not gone to Singapore in 1971 to meet Commonwealth leaders gathering there (although she would like to have done so, she was not invited by the host government; one reason was the problem of setting a precedent, Singapore being a republic) but perhaps this was fortunate since it would be surprising if eventually it does not emerge that the Queen was much out of sympathy with the British Government line to sell arms to South Africa which brought the Commonwealth to the brink of collapse at the conference.

Previous conferences (except for the brief emergency one on Rhodesia in Lagos in January 1966) had been in London and as this is her place of residence any suggestion of her identification with British policy did not arise. But if she had travelled to Singapore she might have found herself in an embarrassing situation. Britain was heavily outnumbered by those opposing her arms policy—many of them countries of which she was also Queen.

But when it was agreed that Commonwealth Heads of Government should meet in Ottawa in 1973 the Queen made it known, even when haggling was going on about the date (principally because Mr Heath was not keen to attend another Commonwealth conference for at least another year) that she would be there whatever date was decided.

She set a new pattern for meetings outside Britain by being on hand to meet all the Heads of Government as they assembled, holding a dinner, talking with each of them individually, and then as the conference opened, departing. She thus in no way identifies herself with the proceedings (which, of course, she never did even in London), and does not declare them open. She followed the same pattern in Jamaica in 1975.

In the case of Ottawa the Queen was able to act as host in her capacity as Queen of Canada and in Kingston she was acting as Queen of Jamaica.

The procedure might have to be slightly altered when the conference is held in a Commonwealth country that is, like Singapore, a republic. But then she would be acting solely in her capacity as Head of the Commonwealth and it is hardly likely in future that any Commonwealth country would put an obstacle in the way of the Head of the Association coming to see them.

The Queen's decision to go to Ottawa and thus to identify herself so strongly with the Commonwealth at what was still a period of controversy can only have been a personal decision taken after consultation with Commonwealth countries and with the then Commonwealth Secretary-General, Mr Arnold Smith. It has been little realized since the Commonwealth Secretariat was set up in 1965 that the Secretary-General, as well as being directly responsible to all the thirty-six Heads of Government, also has direct contact with the Queen as Head of the Commonwealth.

The Ottawa decision meant, even though so many observers after Singapore were prepared to write off the Commonwealth as finished, the Queen was not afraid to proclaim publicly that she at least believed in its future. Her faith was fully justified. Ottawa showed the Commonwealth had begun to settle down into a calmer atmosphere and the Queen was able to push the point home with her television broadcast.

The Commonwealth is very much part of the Queen's daily preoccupation. For example, as part of her routine, she makes sure that if any Commonwealth President or Prime Minister is visiting London top priority is given to making arrangements for him to call on her at Buckingham Palace at least for a talk and more likely for lunch or dinner.

In recent years there have been other ways in which the Queen has indicated her personal feelings about the Commonwealth. In 1965 a multi-faith service was held at St Mary le Bow, Cheapside, during the Commonwealth Arts Festival. The Duke of Edinburgh attended. The event underlined the reality that the vast majority of Commonwealth peoples were non-Christian and inspired the idea that a multi-faith service should be held each Commonwealth Day,* with Hindus, Moslems and peoples of other faiths participating and with the Queen present as Head of the Commonwealth.

A year later the Queen and the Duke attended a Multi-Faith Observance, as it came to be called, at St Martin-in-the-Fields. A similar ceremony in 1967 was cancelled because conservative elements in the Church of England disapproved of leaders of other faiths worshipping in a service held in an Anglican church. For the four years following, the Observance was held in Guildhall. As if to underline her support for the multi-faith concept the Queen attended the 1968 service. In 1972 the Church's objections were finally overcome and the Observance was held in Westminster Abbey with the Queen in attendance. It is now firmly established that the Queen attends the service whenever possible.

This and other actions by the Queen have shown that she is well in tune with thinking in a Commonwealth that consists of 1,000 million people, only 60 million of whom are United Kingdom subjects. Time and again so far as the Commonwealth is concerned it has been Buckingham Palace which has recognized change in advance of politicians and people. Thus we find that it is many years since the Queen referred to the *British* Commonwealth in any public pronouncement, and in Christchurch in 1974 the Duke of Edinburgh found himself arguing with New Zealanders and others who wanted to preserve the title 'The British Commonwealth Games' instead of, as was eventually decided (years after most other institutions had dropped the 'British') calling them 'The Commonwealth Games'.

The Duke, for his part, has always emphasized the constructive co-operation that is carried on by countless Commonwealth

---

* Commonwealth Day, until 1977 celebrated on different days according to the country, is now a permanent fixture throughout the Commonwealth—the second Monday in March.

associations and pointed to the continual increase in this activity. With his Commonwealth Youth Study conferences and his Award scheme, now repeated in several countries (in Kenya it is 'The President's Award Scheme', in Ghana 'The Head of State Award' and so forth), he has contributed practically in building the association—and not, it seems quite clear, for the sake of the prestige of the royal family. The Commonwealth, in any case, has hardly been a popular or fashionable cause in Britain in recent years.

But in the light of the Queen's special role it was not surprising that when, at Kingston, the venue of the next Heads of Government meeting was discussed there was immediate acceptance that it should return to London in mid-1977, in the words of the communiqué, 'at the time of the celebrations of the Silver Jubilee of HM the Queen's accession as Head of the Commonwealth'. Zambia would much have liked the conference in Lusaka and Australia wanted it to be held in Canberra, but both readily agreed this one must be in London.

Today we find that, as the Queen passes her Silver Jubilee, she has developed 'elder statesman' qualities which command respect for her in all Commonwealth countries not as Queen of the United Kingdom but as a person in her own right; she is above the daily political struggle yet in a unique way she has influenced events and played a vital role in keeping the Commonwealth in existence not as an extension of Empire (nor as an extension of Buckingham Palace) but simply because she believes, as do so many others around the world, that it is at the least a useful grouping for nations throughout the world to belong to.

CHAPTER ELEVEN

The Commonwealth in the Year 2000

LESS THAN A quarter of the Twentieth Century is left. It is a short time: much less now, in the industrialized countries, than half a man's lifetime. To put such a period in some perspective I think back forty odd years—to 1935. I recall as a small child, on 6 May of that year, standing at a window of an uncle's office in the Strand—I believe it was somewhere opposite St Clement Danes—watching the Silver Jubilee procession of King George V moving towards St Pauls.

It was a fairy-tale spring morning: the bearded King-Emperor, seated in an open landau, the plumes of his field-marshal's hat fluttering in the breeze; Queen Mary, wearing one of her familiar toques and a white fur cape. Within nine months the King was dead, and within eighteen months a third King reigned.

It was a world of no television, no plastic, no frozen foods. No airliner service flew the Atlantic. Radar and the jet engine and atomic power were many years away. Ideas about orbiting space, sending rockets to Mars and Man walking on the moon were pure space-fiction.

In 1935, though Gandhi was active in India, there was little indication that the pattern of the British Empire would be, another twenty five years later, much different from the vast Victorian, disciplined family it still seemed to be on that May morning.

The gangsterism of Germany and Japan, the obscene horrors of Spain, World War II, and the smaller wars that have followed, the development of air travel to a stage where it is as familiar to us as railway travel, the race in space—all these have crowded since then into little more than forty years.

Nor had the previous decades been much less eventful. A man born in 1900 had by 1935 seen in his lifetime the coming of the aeroplane, the development of the motor-car, a war of dimensions never before dreamed of, a revolution in Russia that had changed the face of the world.

Almost certainly this Twentieth Century pace of events is too fast for the health of the world, but in no way will it halt. One overall prediction about the next twenty-five years we can all make with complete confidence: changes in that period will be just as many and just as traumatic as those which took place between 1900 and the Thirties and between 1930 and the Seventies.

All accurate prophecy, however, ceases at this point. We can only gaze—though that in itself is a useful exercise. Man's actions must in practice be based on what he *believes* is going to happen, in

120

part because most of our actions should be dictated by the way we *want* events to shape.

Shall we want, or need, a Commonwealth in the year 2000? If the answer is yes, we must act in a way that we believe will preserve it and develop it—not on the basis of a prediction that we do not think it will last till then.

As this book has tried to show, great progress has been made in the Commonwealth in the last few years in non-political co-operation. Given the goodwill and encouragement of governments, there is no reason why this work should not be continuing twenty-five years from now on a vastly increased scale. In this event I see a Commonwealth evolving which will be larger and more important that it is today. Many countries of great economic and political potential are within the Commonwealth; India, Canada, Nigeria and Australia will by 2000 AD have assumed more significant inter-national roles than they play today. If South Africa, as the new state of Azania, has rejoined the Commonwealth, as is quite possible, the association should be carrying considerably greater economic weight in the world. One of the Commonwealth's handi-caps so far has been the comparative economic weakness (in world terms) of its richer members.

It is unlikely, though we cannot be certain, that any country of the Commonwealth will by 2000 have the British monarch as its sovereign. Australia, Canada, and New Zealand will in all probability be republics. Some Commonwealth countries may, of course, have their own monarch (as Malaysia has today).

The position of Head of the Commonwealth may have begun to rotate. Thus we could have, for example, an African Head of the Commonwealth, supported by a Malaysian Secretary-General with British and Jamaican assistants.

This will be a world in which people of all creeds and races and nationalities are mixing up at a rapid rate, a world in which it will be possible to travel across the Atlantic in an hour or so, and from Britain to Australia in three hours, a world in which it will be possible to speak by telephone visually direct from London to Sydney, from Delhi to Nairobi. Communication by satellite will have replaced cable links entirely.

The peoples of many of what we now call the developing countries will have produced a large, well-to-do middle class. These people will be touring the world on a huge scale. Parties of Indians and Chinese will be enjoying the beaches of the Mediterranean more and more. British holiday-makers in large numbers will be basking on the beaches of India and Indonesia and Africa.

Intermarrying on a growing scale will be starting to produce the coffee-skinned human being which at some stage in the world's development (500 years hence?) the Creator surely intends the peoples of this globe to become. A Negro will become President of the United States.

It is against this backcloth of tremendous international social upheaval—incredible as it may at first appear to us today, and unwilling as many are to accept it—that we must set the Commonwealth. This is a world backcloth in front of which today's arguments about race in America, about South Africa, about whether a coloured man lives next door to a white man in Brixton will look petty and ridiculous.

The Commonwealth has to go along with this kind of world—indeed it has to blaze a trail ahead of these developments—if it is still to exist in 2000.

The hazards are many on the way. The Commonwealth is not safe yet. The experience of the last two decades, of Singapore and Ottawa, can be of great value in the difficult years still to come; the Commonwealth could still be ignored or cast aside as a result of the emergence of intemperate leadership in one member country or another. The way in which a change of government in New Zealand in 1975 suddenly cast a cloud over the whole future of the most important popular manifestation of the Commonwealth—the Commonwealth Games—showed that storms were still to come.

A fortunate mix of Commonwealth leaders in the early Seventies produced the advance from Singapore and the successful meetings of Ottawa and Kingston—the Commonwealth convert Trudeau, the new-broom leaders Whitlam, Kirk and Rowling in Australia and New Zealand (determined to take their countries out of the post-colonial adolescence), the visionary Manley of Jamaica combined with the experienced Nyerere, Kaunda, Lee Kuan Yew. Britain's Wilson and Heath, each in his own way, had to catch up on the manner in which the Commonwealth had evolved in the Sixties. A move away from old ideas in the developed Commonwealth, particularly in Australia and New Zealand, had coincided with a steadily calmer approach to world affairs on the part of the recently independent developing countries.

If now there is to be a period in which developed countries swing to the right it cannot be assumed—indeed it is hardly likely—that developing countries will move over still further to accommodate them on such subjects as the New International Economic Order or Southern Africa. So far as the Commonwealth is concerned, the litmus remains South Africa itself, as the argument over the 1978 Commonwealth Games showed.

Over the next twenty years or so the Commonwealth will continue to survive—or not—as a result of its handling of issues of race, and in the world today by far the most crucial arena of race conflict is South Africa. No longer a Commonwealth country, its future is nonetheless of burning interest to almost all the member countries of the Commonwealth. To the developing countries racial injustice is being deliberately perpetuated on an ideological basis, and on that score there can be no compromise. To the developed—and particularly to Britain of the four Commonwealth countries in this category—it is a nation of great riches with which there are deep historic and economic links. The South African problem contains the most lethal of all ingredients—great wealth and racial division. Superpower interest in the wealth and in the strategic position of South Africa is bound to grow and so deepen the conflict. Arguably, there is no greater danger to world peace than the South African situation. It is easily within the capability of the countries of the Western world to force change in South Africa within a very few years. A determined and united policy by the United States and the countries of the European Economic Community could not be resisted by the four million Whites of South Africa. If the West worked out a strategy nothing could stop it bringing about African government in South Africa by the mid-Eighties at the latest.

Such a policy is the only sensible one for the West if it wants to pursue and secure a peaceful solution in South Africa. This would forestall Russian involvement and ensure the emergence of a non-aligned Azania that would be in the interests of all mankind.

The West, however, does not seem likely to act in a strong and united manner on this issue; its performance over Rhodesia since 1965 provides no encouragement. However much it may protest to the contrary that it genuinely tried to replace the Smith regime, the undeniable fact is that Western countries kept it going—Portugal, France, Japan, the United States and several more.

The West preferred to live with the Portuguese regimes in Angola and Mozambique rather than to force decolonization in the early Sixties. By dithering over Rhodesia it attracted the activity of those very Communist elements it was so obsessional about keeping out. There is no sign that the West is learning the lesson; the hopes for any peaceful transition of power in South Africa are slim indeed. Nor can there be any real hope that the Afrikaner and British peoples of South Africa will act with greater enlightenment than their Rhodesian brethren did to the north. On the contrary, their line is likely to be harder and they will find plenty of friends in the Western world to support them.

To fulfil short-term needs for chrome the United States was apparently happy to sacrifice long-term Western interests; it could not see, nor did it want to see, that the simple Soviet objective was to make it appear to the world that the West was really on the side of the white man and that it therefore followed that they, the Russians, were the real friends of the black man after all. The Africans had no wish to become pawns in this power game, but they had little alternative. By the end of the Seventies they are in the thick of it.

Without more enlightened and more long-sighted policies from the West the immediate prospect in Southern Africa and therefore on international race relations is unpromising. On past record, the West will prevaricate and dabble, from time to time pretending to do one thing while trying to do another.

No one should be under any illusions that the Soviet Union's intentions are any more honourable than those of the United States. Their eyes are on the resources of Southern Africa, too, and their preoccupation with the West is constant. They also make serious policy mistakes—a fact that people in the West too often overlook—and in the rich-poor economic arguments of the past few years they have not avoided giving the impression that, when it comes to the question of sharing resources on this planet more equally, the Eastern countries are not feeling any more generous to the Third World—in fact rather less so—than the countries of the West. At the end of the day the Soviet Union is a rich white country too.

In the greediness of both sides and their capacity for making mistakes in international policy lies, paradoxically, a hope for the developing countries that they will not be swallowed up by one or the other, but will be able to maintain the separate independent existence that most of them have so far managed to do. For all the many deep bilateral divisions within its one hundred-odd member countries, the astonishing fact about the Non-Aligned Movement founded in 1961 is its ability to identify a number of major issues on which it can agree and to pursue a common line on them.

The continuation of the imperial age, such as existed when George V celebrated his Silver Jubilee, would almost certainly have produced the Third World War we have all been dreading since Hiroshima. The existence of a Third World—as it is loosely, usefully, and inaccurately labelled—of non-aligned countries has prevented that clash and continues to prevent it. The lingering of old imperial notions in places like Southern Africa, however, continues to threaten the tenuous balance.

The idea that non-alignment has already bought the world more than two decades of peace and may buy more decades would be fiercely challenged by many in the West. It is nonetheless probably the case.

True, many states are not properly non-aligned; some like Cuba lean so far to the east that they are all but in the Russian camp; others like Indonesia so far to the West they are all but in the American camp. The great bulk, however, do genuinely play an even-handed role and most of those that seem to lean too far have their own useful influences to exert on one side or the other.

Too much emphasis is laid today on the disorder of the world without proper consideration being given to the new order that has been brought about in the last forty years since World War II with the birth of the United Nations and a great and growing variety of international and regional organizations, all of which have agencies co-operating for the human good. Such bodies as the World Health Organization, which has just scored a historic success with the elimination of smallpox from the face of the earth—an achievement which alone justifies its existence in the last thirty years—and the Food and Agricultural Organization did not exist in 1935. The swift international response for aid to the victims of earthquake, flood and eruption, is a development too often overlooked by public concentration on the inevitably less happy political aspects of international organizations. The UN is seen in terms of bickering in the Security Council Chamber instead of in terms of the much more important battle against smallpox. Newspapers, radio and television have much to answer for by creating this imbalance in the public mind.

At the same time political issues like those involving Southern Africa *are* critical to the world's future and in no way will the Commonwealth be able to avoid deep involvement in these developments, nor should it try do do so. With its links into so many international groupings it could become crucially important in preventing the South African issue from deteriorating into an international political disaster area.

Britain, which wants so much to hope that these problems will somehow just go away, will be deeply implicated because of its business as well as ethnic links. As a country belonging to the EEC and the Commonwealth and having solid links with the United States its diplomatic ingenuity will be taxed to the limit and there is no escape.

As with South Africa so with the New International Economic Order. In the attempt to transfer some of the wealth of the rich world to the poor, the development of more industry in developing countries, the restructuring of the world's financial organizations which has to take place however much the superpowers and the rest of the rich world may resist it, the Commonwealth is likely to play an increasing role.

Whatever difficult and different attitudes are struck up by individual member-countries the value of the Commonwealth will lie as a forum where these views can be exchanged and persuasion applied, where this sample of the world can be the testing ground for new ideas and formulae.

One thing is certain: on past showing, the next thirty years are going to bring dramatic changes. With a Commonwealth, many of the changes could be for the better. Without one, the future could be bleaker.

Appendices

1. List of Commonwealth countries, status and populations.
2. The Divisions of the Commonwealth Secretariat.
3. List of attendance at the four summit conferences 1969-75.
4. Declaration of Commonwealth Principles.
5. New International Economic Order—the two views at Kingston.
6. The Commonwealth Group of Experts. List of names.
7. Aims of the Commonwealth Foundation.
Bibliography

Appendix I
36 NATIONS AND 1,000 MILLION PEOPLE
List of Commonwealth Countries.

Status and Populations

Australia	13 million	M
Bahamas	170,000	M
Bangladesh	70 million	R
Barbados	250,000	M
Botswana	545,000	R
Britain	56 million	M
Canada	21 million	M
Cyprus	610,000	R
Fiji	500,000	M
The Gambia	320,000	R
Ghana	8 million	R
Grenada	100,000	M
Guyana	750,000	R
India	600 million	R
Jamaica	2 million	M
Kenya	10 million	R
Lesotho	1 million	M*
Malawi	4 million	R
Malaysia	10·5 million	M*
Malta	320,000	R
Mauritius	800,000	M
Nauru	6,000	R
New Zealand	2·8 million	M
Nigeria	80 million	R
Papua New Guinea	2 million	M
Seychelles	58,000	R
Sierra Leone	2·5 million	R
Singapore	2 million	R
Sri Lanka	12 million	R
Swaziland	400,000	M
Tanzania	12·5 million	R
Tonga	80,000	M
Trinidad and Tobago	1 million	R
Uganda	8 million	R
Western Samoa	130,000	R
Zambia	4 million	R

Key: R — Republic
M — Monarchy (having Queen Elizabeth as monarch)
M* — Monarchy (having monarch other than Queen Elizabeth)

Appendix II

The Commonwealth Secretariat has the following divisions:

International Affairs
Economic Affairs
Food Production and Rural Development
Education
Legal
Medical Adviser
Scientific Adviser
Applied Studies in Government
Youth
Information
Administration
  Commonwealth Fund for Technical Co-operation (CFTC)
  General Technical Assistance
  Export Market Development
  Education and Training
  Technical Assistance Group

Appendix III

The Full List of Those Present at the Four Summit Meetings
Analysed in Chapters 3-8

LONDON—JANUARY, 1969

AUSTRALIA
John G. Gorton (Prime Minister)

BARBADOS
Errol W. Barrow (Prime Minister and Minister for External Affairs)

BOTSWANA
Sir Seretse Khama (President)

BRITAIN
Harold Wilson (Prime Minister)

CANADA
Pierre Elliott Trudeau (Prime Minister)

CEYLON
Dudley S. Senanayake (Prime Minister)

CYPRUS
Archbishop Makarios (President)

THE GAMBIA
Sir Dawda Jawara (Prime Minister)

GHANA
J. W. K. Harlley (Vice-Chairman, National Liberation Council)

INDIA
Mrs Indira Gandhi (Prime Minister)

JAMAICA
Hugh L. Shearer (Prime Minister and Minister of External Affairs)

KENYA
J. S. Gichuru (Minister of Finance)

LESOTHO
Chief Leabua Jonathan (Prime Minister and Minister for Foreign
Affairs)

MALAWI
Kamuzu Banda (President)

MALAYSIA
Tunku Abdul Rahman Putra Al-Haj (Prime Minister and Minister of Foreign Affairs)

MALTA
Giorgio Borg-Olivier (Prime Minister)

MAURITIUS
Sir Seewoosagur Ramgoolam (Prime Minister and Minister for External Affairs)

NEW ZEALAND
K. J. Holyoake (Prime Minister)

NIGERIA
Chief Obafemi Awolowo (Deputy Chairman, Federal Executive Council and Commissioner for Finance)

PAKISTAN
M. Arshad Husain (Minister for Foreign Affairs)

SIERRA LEONE
Siaka P. Stevens (Prime Minister)

SINGAPORE
Lee Kuan Yew (Prime Minister)

SWAZILAND
Prince Makhosini Dlamini (Prime Minister)

TANZANIA
Julius K. Nyerere (President)

TRINIDAD AND TOBAGO
Dr Eric Williams (Prime Minister)

UGANDA
A. Milton Obote (President)

ZAMBIA
Kenneth Kaunda (President)

SECRETARIAT
Arnold Smith (Secretary-General)

AUSTRALIA
John G. Gorton (Prime Minister)

BARBADOS
Errol W. Barrow (Prime Minister and Minister for External Affairs)

BOTSWANA
Sir Seretse Khama (President)

BRITAIN
Edward Heath (Prime Minister)

CANADA
Pierre Elliott Trudeau (Prime Minister)

CEYLON
Mrs Sirimavo Bandaranaike (Prime Minister)

CYPRUS
Archbishop Makarios (President)

FIJI
Sir Kamisese Mara (Prime Minister)

THE GAMBIA
Sir Dawda Jawara (President)

GHANA
Dr K. A. Busia (Prime Minister)

GUYANA
Forbes Burnham (Prime Minister)

INDIA
Swaran Singh (Foreign Minister)

JAMAICA
Hugh Shearer (Prime Minister and Minister of External Affairs)

KENYA
Daniel Arap Moi (Vice-President and Minister of Home Affairs)

LESOTHO
Chief Leabua Jonathan (Prime Minister and Minister of Foreign Affairs)

MALAWI
Kamuzu Banda (President)

MALAYSIA
Tun Abdul Razak (Prime Minister)

MALTA
Giorgio Borg-Olivier (Prime Minister and Minister of Commonwealth and Foreign Affairs)

MAURITIUS
Sir Seewoosagur Ramgoolam (Prime Minister)

NEW ZEALAND
Sir Keith Holyoake (Prime Minister)

NIGERIA
Okoi Arikpo (Commissioner for External Affairs)

PAKISTAN
Ahsanul Haque (Minister of Commerce)

SIERRA LEONE
C. P. Foray (Minister of External Affairs)

SINGAPORE
Lee Kuan Yew (Prime Minister)

SWAZILAND
Prince Makhosini Dlamini (Prime Minister)

TANZANIA
Julius K. Nyerere (President)

TONGA
Prince Tu'ipelehake (Prime Minister and Minister for Foreign Affairs)

TRINIDAD AND TOBAGO
Karl T. Hudson-Phillips (Attorney-General and Minister for Legal Affairs)

UGANDA
A. Milton Obote (President)

WESTERN SAMOA
Tupua Tamasese Lealofi IV (Prime Minister)

ZAMBIA
Kenneth Kaunda (President)

SECRETARIAT
Arnold Smith (Secretary-General)

AUSTRALIA
E. G. Whitlam (Prime Minister)

THE BAHAMAS
Lynden O. Pindling (Prime Minister)

BANGLADESH
Sheikh Mujibur Rahman (Prime Minister)

BARBADOS
Errol W. Barrow (Prime Minister)

BOTSWANA
Sir Seretse Khama (President)

BRITAIN
Edward Heath (Prime Minister)

CANADA
Pierre Elliott Trudeau (Prime Minister)

CYPRUS
John Cl. Christophides (Foreign Minister)

FIJI
Sir Kamisese Mara (Prime Minister and Minister for Foreign Affairs)

THE GAMBIA
Andrew Camara (Vice-President and Minister of External Affairs)

GHANA
Brigadier N. Y. R. Ashley-Lassen (Member of the National Redemption Council and Chief of Defence Staff)

GUYANA
Forbes Burnham (Prime Minister)

INDIA
Swaran Singh (Foreign Minister)

JAMAICA
Michael Manley (Prime Minister)

KENYA
Daniel Arap Moi (Vice-President and Minister for Home Affairs)

LESOTHO
Chief Leabua Jonathan (Prime Minister)

MALAWI
J. D. Msonthi (Minister of Education)

MALAYSIA
Tun Abdul Razak (Prime Minister)

MALTA
Dom Mintoff (Prime Minister)

MAURITIUS
Sir Seewoosagur Ramgoolam (Prime Minister)

NEW ZEALAND
Norman E. Kirk (Prime Minister)

NIGERIA
General Yakubu Gowon (Head of the Federal Military Government)

SIERRA LEONE
Siaka Stevens (President)

SINGAPORE
Lee Kuan Yew (Prime Minister)

SRI LANKA
Mrs Sirimavo Bandaranaike (Prime Minister)

SWAZILAND
Prince Makhosini J. Dlamini (Prime Minister)

TANZANIA
Julius K. Nyerere (President)

TONGA
Prince Tu'ipelehake (Prime Minister)

TRINIDAD AND TOBAGO
Francis Prevatt (Minister of Petroleum and Mines)

UGANDA
P. O. Etiang (Acting Minister for Foreign Affairs)

WESTERN SAMOA
Fiame Mata'afa Faumuina Mulinu'u II (Prime Minister)

ZAMBIA
Mainza Chona (Vice-President)

SECRETARIAT
Arnold Smith (Secretary-General)

AUSTRALIA
E. G. Whitlam (Prime Minister)
THE BAHAMAS
Lynden O. Pindling (Prime Minister)
BANGLADESH
Sheikh Mujibur Rahman (President)
BARBADOS
Errol W. Barrow (Prime Minister)
BOTSWANA
Sir Seretse Khama (President)
BRITAIN
Harold Wilson (Prime Minister)
CANADA
Pierre Elliott Trudeau (Prime Minister)
CYPRUS
Archbishop Makarios (President)
FIJI
Sir Kamisese Mara (Prime Minister)
THE GAMBIA
Sir Dawda Jawara (President)
GHANA
Lt-Col Kwame Baah (Commissioner for Foreign Affairs)
GRENADA
Eric Gairy (Prime Minister)
GUYANA
Forbes Burnham (Prime Minister)
INDIA
Mrs Indira Gandhi (Prime Minister)
JAMAICA
Michael Manley (Prime Minister and Minister of External Affairs)
KENYA
Daniel Arap Moi (Vice-President and Minister for Home Affairs)
LESOTHO
Chief Leabua Jonathan (Prime Minister)
MALAWI
D. T. Matenje (Minister of Finance, Trade, Industry and Tourism)
MALAYSIA
Tun Abdul Razak (Prime Minister)
MALTA
Dom Mintoff (Prime Minister)

MAURITIUS
Sir Seewoosagur Ramgoolam (Prime Minister)
NEW ZEALAND
W. E. Rowling (Prime Minister)
NIGERIA
General Yakubu Gowon (Head of Federal Military Government)
SIERRA LEONE
Siaka Stevens (President)
SINGAPORE
Lee Kuan Yew (Prime Minister)
SRI LANKA
Mrs Sirimavo Bandaranaike (Prime Minister)
SWAZILAND
Prince Makhosini Dlamini (Prime Minister)
TANZANIA
Julius K. Nyerere (President)
TONGA
Prince Tu'ipelehake (Prime Minister)
TRINIDAD AND TOBAGO
K. Mohammed (Minister of Health and Leader of the House of Representatives)
UGANDA
K. Y. Kinene (Permanent Representative to the UN)
WESTERN SAMOA
Fiame Mata'afa Faumuina Mulinu'u II (Prime Minister)
ZAMBIA
Kenneth Kaunda (President)
SECRETARIAT
Arnold Smith (Secretary-General)

Appendix IV

See Chapter 5

On 22 January 1971, at their meeting in Singapore, Commonwealth Heads of Government unanimously approved the following Declaration of Commonwealth Principles:

The Commonwealth of Nations is a voluntary association of independent sovereign states, each responsible for its own policies, consulting and co-operating in the common interests of their peoples and in the promotion of international understanding and world peace.

Members of the Commonwealth come from territories in the six continents and five oceans, include peoples of different races, languages and religions, and display every stage of economic development from poor developing nations to wealthy industrialized nations. They encompass a rich variety of cultures, traditions and institutions.

Membership of the Commonwealth is compatible with the freedom of member governments to be non-aligned or to belong to any other grouping, association or alliance. Within this diversity all members of the Commonwealth hold certain principles in common. It is by pursuing these principles that the Commonwealth can continue to influence international society for the benefit of mankind.

We believe that international peace and order are essential to the security and prosperity of mankind; we therefore support the United Nations and seek to strengthen its influence for peace in the world, and its efforts to remove the causes of tension between nations.

We believe in the liberty of the individual, in equal rights for all citizens regardless of race, colour, creed or political belief, and in their inalienable right to participate by means of free and democratic political processes in framing the society in which they live. We therefore strive to promote in each of our countries those representative institutions and guarantees for personal freedom under the law that are our common heritage.

We recognize racial prejudice as a dangerous sickness threatening the healthy development of the human race and racial discrimination as an unmitigated evil of society. Each of us will vigorously combat this evil within our own nation.

No country will afford to regimes which practise racial discrimination assistance which in its own judgement directly contributes to the pursuit or consolidation of this evil policy. We oppose all forms of colonial domination and racial oppression and are committed to the principles of human dignity and equality.

We will therefore use all our efforts to foster human equality and dignity everywhere, and to further the principles of self-determination and non-racialism.

We believe that the wide disparities in wealth now existing between different sections of mankind are too great to be tolerated. They also create world tensions. Our aim is their progressive removal. We therefore seek to use our efforts to overcome poverty, ignorance and disease, in raising standards of life and achieving a more equitable international society.

To this end our aim is to achieve the freest possible flow of international trade on terms fair and equitable to all, taking into account the special requirements of the developing countries, and to encourage the flow of adequate resources, including governmental and private resources, to the developing countries, bearing in mind the importance of doing this in a true spirit of partnership and of establishing for this purpose in the developing countries conditions which are conducive to sustained investment and growth.

We believe that international co-operation is essential to remove the causes of war, promote tolerance, combat injustice, and secure development among the peoples of the world. We are convinced that the Commonwealth is one of the most fruitful associations for these purposes.

In pursuing these principles the members of the Commonwealth believe that they can provide a constructive example of the multinational approach which is vital to peace and progress in the modern world. The association is based on consultation, discussion and co-operation.

In rejecting coercion as an instrument of policy they recognize that the security of each member state from external aggression is a matter of concern to all members. It provides many channels for continuing exchanges of knowledge and views on professional, cultural, economic, legal and political issues among member states.

These relationships we intend to foster and extend, for we believe that our multi-national association can expand human understanding and understanding among nations, assist in the elimination of discrimination based on differences of race, colour or creed, maintain and strengthen personal liberty, contribute to the enrichment of life for all, and provide a powerful influence for peace among nations.

Appendix V

See Chapter 8

The two views on the New International Economic Order are summed up by the following extracts from the speeches of Forbes Burnham, Prime Minister of Guyana, and Harold Wilson, Prime Minister of Britain.

FORBES BURNHAM:

1. It will not do to deceive ourselves about the nature of the task which must be attempted. We must embark on building a new order. It is not a task for the repair or renovation or the piece-meal reconstruction of the old order. The sharp rise in petroleum prices did not precipitate the crisis of change. It illuminated its dimensions and its inter-related aspects.

2. The new international economic order must be predicated upon an international economic environment which is capable of accommodating different economic and social systems. Moreover, we should not talk about commodities without talking about the transfer of real resources, without talking about the transnational corporations and the transfer of technology and without recognizing the urgent need for the reform and restructuring of the appropriate international institutions and the critical role that must be played by the international monetary and financial system on which I hope others in this debate will enlarge.

3. There is another danger that needs to be guarded against if we are all serious in our commitment to programmes of positive action which will give life to a new international economic order. It is the danger of deceiving ourselves that we can somehow achieve fundamental change by marginal adjustments and devices of a piecemeal and reformist nature. This is not to say that there is no value in particular approaches. It is to emphasize that we will not make real progress unless we evolve an integrated programme designed to fulfil not merely the aspirations of the developing world but the necessities for survival of the global community.

HAROLD WILSON's six points for action:

1. To establish better exchanges of information on forward supply and demand.

2. To elaborate more specific rules to define the circumstances under which import and export restrictions may be applied to commodities.

141

3. To encourage the development of producer/consumer associations for individual commodities.

4. To give fresh impetus to the joint efforts of producers and consumers to conclude commodity agreements designed to facilitate the orderly conduct and development of trade. This could be done:

first, by identifying commodities appropriate to the conclusion of such agreements;

second, by analysing commodity by commodity the appropriate mechanism for the regulation of trade within the framework of such agreements (including international buffer stocks, co-ordination of nationally held stocks, production controls and export quotas);

third, by examining ways in which any financial burden arising from these mechanisms, may be appropriately financed.

5. To agree that the regulatory mechanisms incorporated in any international commodity agreement would be directed towards the maintenance of market prices within a range negotiated in accordance with the principles enshrined in the fourth Central Commitment.

6. To establish the framework of a scheme for the stabilisation of export earnings from commodities.

Appendix VI

See Chapter 8

The ten men chosen to form the Commonwealth Group of Experts on the New International Economic Order after the Kingston meeting were:

Alister McIntyre (Grenada). Chairman of the Caribbean Community.

L. Smith (Canada). High Commissioner to several Caribbean states.

Prof. H. M. A. Onitiri (Nigeria). Director-General of Social and Economic Research, Ibadan.

Prof. A. B. Brownlie (New Zealand). Chairman of New Zealand Monetary and Economic Council.

Prof. Nurul Islam (Bangladesh). Deputy Chairman, Bangladesh Planning Commission.

Amir Jamal (Tanzania). Minister for Commerce and Industry.

P. Lai (Malaysia). Permanent Representative to the UN bodies in Geneva. Chairman of GATT Council of Representatives.

L. M. Lishomwa (Zambia). Special assistant (economic) to the President.

Sir Donald Maitland (Britain). Deputy Under-Secretary of State, Foreign and Commonwealth Office.*

Shri S. S. Marathe (India). Bureau of Industrial Costs and Prices.

---

* Replaced late in 1975 by Sidney Golt, Former Deputy Secretary, Board of Trade, Former Leader, UK Delegation to UNCTAD.

Appendix VII

See Chapter 9

The aims of the Commonwealth Foundation were well summed up by Mr John Chadwick, its Director, in a lecture to the Royal Society of Arts in London on 13 May 1976. These are extracts:

'. . . it is fascinating to find—and this reflects our allotted task of helping to 'de-anglicize' the Commonwealth—that the Librarians now have their headquarters in Jamaica: while the Commonwealth Council of Educational Administration works from the University of Armidale, NSW. The secretariat of the Association of Commonwealth Literature has passed, not without some adventures en route, from Ottawa via Kampala to Mysore, while the Commonwealth Legal Bureau and Commonwealth Veterinary Association still function actively from Ontario.

'. . . each pan-Commonwealth Association has played its part in bringing into being new national bodies in smaller countries where none previously existed: in spreading professional know-how and experience: in promoting Commonwealth-wide and regional co-operation, and in advising governments, universities and technical schools, from a collective Commonwealth viewpoint, on such vital matters as standards, ethics, reciprocity, training and retraining and on the introduction of new courses at professional and technician level; on the revision of textbooks and curricula to suit local needs etc. An existing freemasonry of practice and behaviour has thus been constantly adapted so that the professions of today throughout the Commonwealth can attune themselves to society's changing needs. In this process countries both new and old have contributed their equal shares.

'Next . . . the creation of national Professional Centres. There are now thirteen of these in being or formation. They range from the capitals of Guyana, Trinidad and Tobago, Jamaica, Barbados, through Malta to Uganda, Kenya, Zambia and Mauritius and on via Sri Lanka to Malaysia, Singapore and Fiji. Ghana, Nigeria and The Bahamas are other countries where the concept has taken root.

'. . . aid to the individual—in particular to the younger man or woman working in physical or intellectual isolation—has been one of the major concerns of our Trustees. Such help, which extends increasingly far down the sub-professional ladder, may take the form of attendance at a conference or seminar, or for a short courses or study visits elsewhere in the Commonwealth. By now well over 2,000 Commonwealth citizens have broadened their experiences and skills in this way to both their own and their country's benefit. Small sums of money judiciously applied in areas such as this can, we have found, pay handsome dividends.

'Then there is the series of travelling bursary schemes . . . often in fruitful collaboration with learned bodies such as the Royal Society, the Ontario Veterinary College, the Association of Commonwealth Universities of the Agricultural Institute of Canada. A number of such projects, which have also included fire engineers and civil servants in Commonwealth Africa, are helping to promote intra-Commonwealth exchanges of people and ideas in fields which, until now, had barely been considered.

'Or again there is the Commonwealth Foundation Lectureship Programme. Under this some three distinguished professional leaders are invited each year to visit a region of the Commonwealth and to talk, meet with and listen to people in their own field in and out of government. Among topics for such Lectureships have been animal breeding, geology, industrial chemistry, pollution, orthopaedic surgery and the conservation of historic towns and monuments in Africa.

'Professional journals too have proved to be a field where the Foundation could without effort spend all and more than it receives. Here, apart from grants for the supply of existing publications to newly formed professional bodies, we are rather proud of our share in helping to launch and sustain three entirely new basic journals of prime benefit to the newer world, namely *Tropical Doctor*: *Tropical Animal Health and Production* and—more recently—*Appropriate Technology*. All are now well on the road to self-sufficiency.'

BIBLIOGRAPHICAL NOTE

So far few books analyse recent political developments in the Commonwealth.

Survey of Commonwealth Affairs by J. D. B. Miller (Oxford University Press, 1974) deals with the Sixties and takes into account the Singapore conference of 1971.

Earlier developments are documented in The Commonwealth Experience by Nicholas Mansergh (Weidenfeld and Nicolson, 1969).

Empire to Commonwealth 1919 to 1970 by J. B. Watson (J. M. Dent, 1971) records the main developments of the period.

The 'Open' Commonwealth by M. Margaret Ball (Duke University Press, 1971) explores the workings and significance of the Commonwealth with insight and understanding.

Commonwealth by H. Duncan Hall (Van Nostrand Reinhold Co., 1971) is a comprehensive history of the Commonwealth in the first sixty years of this century.

The Modern Commonwealth by Andrew Walker (Longman, 1975) is for younger readers, but is nonetheless a compendium of information valuable as reference for readers of all ages.

The most up-to-date factual information about the Commonwealth is to be obtained from the Commonwealth Secretariat, Pall Mall, London.

Recommended are:

Reference papers on the Commonwealth Secretariat, the Commonwealth Fund for Technical Cooperation and the Commonwealth Foundation. Also the reports of the Experts' Group 'Towards a New International Economic Order' and booklets on the Reform of the International Monetary System, Terms of Trade Policy for Primary Commodities, and Aid and the Commonwealth. Secretariat booklets are available on education in the Commonwealth (Education Research, Provision for Handicapped Children in the Commonwealth Developing Countries, Mathematics Teaching etc.). Other booklets deal with Youth and Development in Asia and the pacific, Africa, Malta and Cyprus, and on Youth Employment Problems.

The reports of the Commonwealth Secretary-General, issued bi-ennially, and of the Director of the Commonwealth Foundation give a full insight into many aspects of Commonwealth activity.

A book giving a full list of Commonwealth Professional Associations was produced by the Commonwealth Foundation in 1976.

Excellent lists of Commonwealth reading matter are produced by
the Commonwealth Institute, Kensington High Street; the National
Book League, Albemarle Street; and the Royal Commonwealth
Society Library, Northumberland Avenue, all in London.

INDEX

academics, role of, 105-8
accountants, 109
Accra, public examinations seminar, 70
Acheampong, Col. I.K., 75, 78, 94
Aden, 113
Adu, A. L. (Yaw), 105
African
  arms sales, opposition by leaders, 61
  Asians, Gowon's view on expulsion, 84
  attitude, new, to Commonwealth, 34
  Indian communities, 63
  Lomé Convention, representation, 22
  majority rule, aim of, 3
  withdrawal, threats of, 51, 53
African Caribbean and Pacific countries (ACP), 91
Africans, training of, from Zimbabwe and Namibia, 97
agricultural development, 4
aid
  and planning conference, 31
  humanitarian, 87
  Lester Pearson Committee on, 83
  technical, 20, 64, 67, 83, 97
Amchitka nuclear testing, 87
Amery, L. S., 15
Amin, Idi, President, 73, 75, 78, 94
Ankrah, Maj. Gen., 29, 36
Anyaoku Ameka, 95
Appropriate Technology, 145
architects, 104
Arikpo, Okoi, 58, 133
arms, freedom fighters, for, 97
arms sales
  British policy, Commonwealth, effect on, 61, 62, 114
  Conservative government's intended, 6, 19, 50-4, 56, 58
  Singapore summit dominated by, 67
  squeeze on, 97
Arusha, Regional Health bureau, 23
Ashley-Lassen, Brig. NYR, 134
Association of South East Asian Nations (ASEAN), 9, 10, 79, 105
Attlee, Clement, 72
auditors-general, meetings of, 31
Australia
  Britain, relationship with, 30, 31
  CFTC, joins, 68
  Commonwealth,
    indifference to, 30, 31, 51, 62
    new attitude to, 8, 77

foreign policy, 8
imperial Commonwealth, picture of, 8
original member, 5
population and status, 128
Rhodesian problem, attitude to, 75
Secretariat, demand for, 14-16
See also Menzies, Sir Robert; Whitlam, E. Gough
Award Schemes, 117
Awolowo, Chief Obafemi, 38, 131
Ayub Khan, President, 27, 33, 36
Azania, 121, 123

Baah, Lt. Col. Kwame, 136
Bahamas, population and status, 128
Banda, Kamuzu, President, London summit, at, 131
  Rhodesian problem, attitude, 29, 36
  Singapore summit, at, 57, 132
Bandaranaike, Mrs Sirimavo, 57, 132, 135, 137
Bangladesh
  Commonwealth, accession to, 21, 60, 64
  establishment of, 64
  export programme, help in, 68
  population and status, 128
  recognition by Britain, 20
  technical aid, 20
bankers, 64, 109
Barbados, 21, 27, 28, 85, 128
Barrow, Errol W., 81, 85, 130, 132, 134, 136
Belize, independence of, 8, 99
Bermuda, 8
Bhutto, President, 20
Biafra, 38
Blantyre, school for teachers of deaf, 104
book development programme, 23, 39
Borg-Olivier, Giorgio, 131, 133
Botswana,
  Commonwealth, benefits from, 62
  majority rule, and, 2
  population and status, 128
  Rhodesia, attitude to, 75
brain drain, 92, 109
Bridgetown, Barbados, 28, 104
Britain
  arms sales, *see* arms sales
  Australia, relationship with, 30, 31
  British Asians problem, 73, 74

148

Commonwealth—continued
Heads of government meetings, *see* summit conferences
imperfect, conception of, 50
imperial preference, decline of, 7
India
  attitudes of, 30, 51, 63, 64
  key position of, 30
  wide cultural connections of, 63
Indo-Pakistan problem, 24, 64, 66
information, need and programme, 32, 39, 69,146, 147
International
  affairs, increasing influence in, 9
  association, independent states, 9, 18, 138
  co-operation, 139
  economic order, importance to new, 11
  position papers, service of, 62
Labour Party, attitude of, 3, 32
liberty, belief in, 138
Macmillan, Harold, attitude of, 32
magnitude, 61, 90, 116
manipulation, early, by Britain, 2
membership, 3, 26
migration, 38, 66
monarchies, 128
multinational approach of, 139
Namibia, possible member, 92
nature, 2
new, 30, 62
New Zealand
  attitude of, 77
  leading role, 62
Nigerian Civil war, 20, 29, 37-8, 51, 66
Non-Aligned Movement, membership in, 10, 138
non-political co-operation, *see* non-political co-operation
numerical strength, 52
Nyerere's concern for, 30
OAS, members in, 10
OAU, members in, 9
Office, 33
old, 30, 72, 79,
Pakistan
  benefits lost by, 64
  withdrawal, 20, 60, 64
Paris North-South dialogue talks, 9
peace, influence for, 138, 140
phenomenon of, 45
philosophy, discussion of, 26, 121-6,
political
  differences with Britain, 113

mood, 7, 10
population movement problem, 66
  statistics, 128
postal agreement, 64
potential of existing members, 121
poverty, attitude to, 139
Powell, Enoch, views, 46
practical nature of, 11
present, 8, 90
preservation of, 18, 19, 53, 58
press, *see* press
Principles, Declaration of Commonwealth, 138
problem
  growth, of, 55
  members, 62
professional co-operation, *see* professional
progress, 80
publicity, 31, 69
purpose, 2
quarrel with Britain not quarrel with, 18
Queen Elizabeth II, *see* Queen Elizabeth II
racial prejudice, opposition to, 138, 139
regional arrangements, *see* regional
relationships, 3, 18, 30
representative institutions, promotion of, 138
republics as members, 63, 113, 128
Rhodesia, *see* Rhodesia
role, 103, 104
Secretariat, *see* Secretariat, Commonwealth
Secretary-General, see Smith, Arnold; Ramphal, Shridath
short-term political ideas excluded, 33
Southern African problem, *see* Southern African
South Pacific forum, members in, 9
sovereignty, loss of, 60, 61
status
  allowed before recognition, 21
  membership countries, of, 128
study and exchange of experience, programme, 23
summit conferences, *see* summit conferences
survival after total changes, 65
technical aid, 24, 64, 67, 83, 97
trade
  flow, 139
  patterns, 7

153

154

155

Makarios, President, 33, 83, 95, 130, 132, 136
Malawi, 112, 128
Malaya, war in, 113
Malaysia
  monarchical system of, 113
  population and status, 128
Malta
  Commonwealth professional centre, 104
  international control of seabed, study, 39
  population and status, 128
Manila, World Bank meeting, 100
Manley, Michael
  Kingston summit, host at, 93-7, 136
    impressive Chairman, 97
  Ottawa summit, at, 78, 82, 90, 134
  pro-African, 75
  rich-poor gap, on, 83, 95
manpower planning, 68
Mara, Sir Kamisese, 134, 136
Maratha, Shri S. S., 143
Margai, Albert, 29, 35
market
  prices, 142
  research, 80
mass communications study, 39
Matenje, D. T., 136
mathematics teaching, 23
Mau Mau, 113
Mauritius, 63, 128
media, new, role of, 32
Medical, Third Conference, 70
medicine, 64
Menzies, Sir Robert
  Australian picture of Commonwealth, and, 8
  Commonwealth, adverse attitude to, 77
  Secretariat, continued demand for, 16
metrication conference, 70
Middle East problems, 80, 90
migration
  countries concerned with, 38
  problem of, 66
  talks on, 38
mineral
  exploitation, 68
  riches on seabed, 63
Mintoff, Dom, 78, 94, 135, 136
Mohammed, K., 137
Moi, Daniel Arap, 132, 134, 136
monarchies, 121, 128
monetary questions, 80, 85, 141

Montserrat, 8
Morning Star, 45
Moslems, 116
Mountbatten, Earl, 113
Mozambique, aid on closing Rhodesian border, 97
Msonthi, J. D., 135
Multi-Faith Observances, 116
multinational companies
  Australian view on, 85
  developed countries, involvement of, 86
  Japanese, British, American, 86
  role of, 23, 141
  security aspect, 86
Muzorewa, Bishop, 95

Nairobi
  Commonwealth professional centre, 104
  economic planners' conference, 22
  planning conference, 31
  UNCTAD 4, 99
  youth study conference, 66
Namibia, 8, 92, 97
national
  development, 106
  interest, 6
Nauru, population and status, 128
Nehru, Jawaharlal, 18
New Commonwealth, benefits accruing to, 62
New Delhi, 40, 70
Newfoundland, Imperial Conference, 1907, 14
New International Economic Order, *see* economic
New Zealand
  Commonwealth, leading role in, 62
  foreign affairs, attitude to, 8
  Imperial Conference, 1907, 14
  nuclear testing, and, 87
  original member, 5
  population and status, 128
  Rhodesian problem, attitude to, 75
  Secretariat, attitude to proposed, 14, 15
NIBMAR (no independence before majority rule), 37
Nigeria
  assassination of Prime Minister, 24
  Britain, importance to, 75
  civil war, 20, 29, 37-8, 51, 66
  delegations, Federal and Biafran, at Kampala, 20
  population and status, 128

157

159

research, 39
resources, transfer of, 141
Rhodesia
  Africans
    attitude to, 5, 37, 75
    training of, 92
  assessment, 123, 124
  border closure, 68
  British manoeuvring, failure of, 4
  Commonwealth relations, effect on, 16, 31
  conference on, Lagos, 114
  continuing issue, 18, 26, 51
  Gowon, General, in debate on, 83
  Kingston summit report, 91
  Mozambique, aid for, on frontier closure, 97
  NIBMAR (no independence before majority rule), 37
  Ottawa summit, significance, 81, 85
  Pearce Commission, 74
  popular interest in problem, 67
  Smith-Home agreement, 74
  speculation on effect on summit, 44-6
  Wilson, Harold, and, 32, 38, 46
  Zimbabwe
    acceptance of name, 97
    potential member of Commonwealth, 8
rich and poor, 83, 85, 90, 95, 139
Richardson, Sir Egerton, 105, 106
rich countries, indexation, against, 91
Rome, Treaty of, 7
Rowling, Wallace, 8, 95, 98, 137
Royal Society, 145
Rupununi uprising, 36
rural
  areas, education in, 32
  development, 23
Russia, see Soviet

Saba Saba celebrations, 21
St Kitts-Nevis, 8
St Lucia, 8
St Vincent, 8
San Francisco Conference, 1945, 44
Scandinavian countries, humanitarian aid of, 87
Scholarship and Fellowship plan, 64
scientific journals, 70
scientists, 104
seabed, international control of, 39, 63
Secretariat, Commonwealth
  administration removed from Whitehall, 4

African issues, relations with Britain over, 18
arms sales, counsel on, 19
assessment of first decade, 23
Australia
  presses for separate, 15
  reservations of, 16
Bangladesh, technical aid to, 20
briefings, 40, 41
British
  attitude to, 33
  West Indies Airways, and, 21
Canada
  attitude of, 15, 16
  important role of, 24
Caribbean Development Bank, and, 21
civil servants, international, as, 23, 36
clearing house, merely, as, 15, 17
Commonwealth officials, organization of conferences for, 22
continued demand for, 16
developing ideas of, 37
diplomacy as vital function, 17, 18
Divisions, 131
Douglas-Home, supported by, 16
early proposals, 14
economic advice, 62
executive functions, not to arrogate to self, 17
Food Production and Rural Development Division, 23, 91, 129
formal procedures, disadvantage of, 17
functional co-operation, 17, 22
Heads, need for representation by, 29, 35, 40, 78
immigration problems, 38
Imperial
  Conference, 1907, proposed at, 14
  War Cabinet, for, 15
independence of members, 21
informality and flexibility, 24
information
  amassing of, 65, 146
  division, need for, 32
initial role, 17
International Affairs Division, 95, 129
Memorandum, agreed on, 17
Mozambique liberation movement, furthering, 21
Namibia, training plan, 92
New Zealand presses for separate, 15
Nigeria civil war, and, 20

161

162

163

SEP 7 - 1979 ✓

DA   INGRAM, DEREK.
4   THE IMPERFECT COMMON-
I53   WEALTH.
1977
c.1

DA   INGRAM, DEREK.
4   THE IMPERFECT COMMONWEALTH.
I53
1977
c.1